Israel and Babylon

Israel and Babylon

The Babylonian Influence on Israelite Religion

HERMANN GUNKEL

Edited with a New Foreword, Notes, and Bibliography
by K. C. Hanson

Translated by E. S. B. and K. C. Hanson

CASCADE *Books* · Eugene, Oregon

ISRAEL AND BABYLON
The Babylonian Influence on Israelite Religion

Cascade Books
A Division of Wipf and Stock Publishers
199 W. 8th Ave., Suite 3
Eugene, OR 97401

www.wipfandstock.com

ISBN 13: 978-1-60608-250-8

Cataloging-in-Publication data:

Gunkel, Hermann, 1862–1932.

    Israel and Babylon : the Babylonian influence on Israelite religion /
Hermann Gunkel. Edited with a New Foreword, Notes, and Bibliography
by K. C. Hanson. Translated by E. S. B. and K. C. Hanson.

    ISBN 13: 978-1-60608-250-8

    xviii + 78 p. ; 20 cm. Includes bibliographical references and indexes.

    Translation of Israel und Babylonien.

    1. Delitzsch, Friedrich, 1850–1922. Babel und Bibel. 2. Assyro-Babylonian
literature—Relation to the Old Testament. 3. Literature, comparative—
Hebrew and Assyro-Babylonian. 4. Judaism—History—To 70 C.E.
I. Hanson, K. C. (Kenneth Charles). II. E. S. B. III. Title.

BS1180 G87 2009

Contents

Illustrations

Photo credits: Ishtar Gate © K. C. Hanson 2000, used by permmission. All others from Robert William Rogers, *Cuneiform Parallels to the Old Testament*.

Foreword

Delitzsch and the Babel–Bible Controversy

The controversy over the relationship between Babylon and Israel was initiated by lectures delivered in January and February 1902, January 1903, and October 1904 by Professor Friedrich Delitzsch (1850–1922). The major reactions to these lectures were due in large part to Delitzsch's delivering the first two lectures at the Deutsche Orient-Gesellschaft (German Oriental Society), with Kaiser Wilhelm II, the emperor's wife, and members of the royal court in attendance. He gave the third lecture at literary societies in Barmen and Köln. The controversy became so widespread that it even garnered its own name: in German "Der Babel-Bibel Streit," and in English "the Babel–Bible Controversy."[1]

Friedrich Delitzsch was the son of the Old Testament scholar Franz Delitzsch (1813–1890). The elder Delitzsch was well known for the series of commentaries he coauthored

---

1. See the third section of the bibliography on the Babel-Bible Controversy below, 70–72.

with C. F. Keil;[2] and while conservative, he was not a fundamentalist. The younger Delitzsch made his reputation as a prominent Assyriologist and Sumerologist, trained by the eminent Eberhard Schrader at the University of Berlin. At the time of his lectures, he was Professor of Assyriology at the University of Berlin and curator of the Western Asiatic collection of the Royal Museum (1899–1919).

The controversy stirred up by Delitzsch's lectures was due in part to the sensational manner in which he framed his conclusions. Rather than simply reporting on the advances in Assyriology, the new documents excavated, and the light they shed on the ancient Near East, he put forth his position that the comparisons between the Babylonian documents and the Old Testament demonstrated that Israel had substantially obtained its literature from Babylon. And regarding many of his comparisons, he argued that the Babylonian forms were superior and the Israelite forms pale imitations. He employed his knowledge of the ancient Near East to characterize the Old Testament as inferior, naive, derivative. Years later Delitzsch developed these views even further in his book *Die grosse Täuschung* (*The Great Deception*). As Shavit and Eran summarize:

> Not only did Delitzsch take to extremes the view that parallels between the culture of Babylonia and the Bible attested to the fact that a large part of the biblical world was borrowed from Babylonia, nor was he content to describe Babylonia one spiritual level higher than that of ancient Israel, presenting the Babylonian culture as a model of law, ethics

2. Keil and Delitzsch, *Biblical Commentary on the Old Testament*, 25 vols.

and justice. Thus he turned "sinful Babylon," the city that, in the world of Christianity, symbolized vainglory, sin and evil, into the ancient source of Christian values and Western civilization—all via its influence on Greek culture and Christianity. Babylonia, now enjoying a renaissance, was depicted as a developed, advanced culture worthy of admiration for its estimable qualities, a culture that influenced the entire region in whose center it dwelled, and even beyond that, a culture whose literature—and not the Bible—represented the values of humanistic-universal ethics.[3]

Gunkel acknowledged Delitzsch's talent and reputation in the field of Assyriology. Delitzsch was a respected Semitist, well versed in ancient Near Eastern documents and languages. He was correct in making comparisons between Babylon and Israel in terms of both general cultural issues as well as religion, especially given Babylon's centuries of influence throughout the ancient Near East and the Judeans' exile to Babylon in the sixth century BCE. But despite these acknowledgments, Gunkel felt compelled to publish this small volume to expose what he considered Delitzsch's polemical attitude and serious flaws of method and logic. Gunkel's critique includes the following key points:

- Delitzsch unfortunately treated the comparisons between Babylon and Israel in a cavalier manner, often with polemical interests.

- He misinterpreted numerous biblical passages—at times not taking genre into account (such as the

3. Shavit and Eran, *The Hebrew Bible Reborn*, 212.

folktale), and at others simply misrepresenting the Hebrew text.

- He interpreted relationships between ancient texts solely in scribal terms, failing to take centuries of oral tradition into account.

- He demonstrated no awareness of the methods of the history of religion (*Religionsgeschichte*); Gunkel was a renowned leader in "the History of Religion School" (*die Religionsgeschichtliche Schule*).

- His understanding of modern theology, especially with regard to the issue of revelation, was superficial, naïve, and uninformed by the current theological discussion.

But the controversy was also fueled by other considerations as well. Because the first two lectures were held at meetings of the Deutsche Orient-Gesellschaft, with the kaiser and members of his court in attendance, they received much more newspaper coverage than they would if they had been simply university lectures. As Gunkel points out, the newspapers also stoked the controversy because of its potential for scandal and controversy. But Gunkel also observes that the general ignorance of the public about ancient Near Eastern and biblical issues made them easy targets for the newspapers' headlines.

A Comparative Approach in the Twenty-first Century

Where do things stand after a century of research in Assyriology and the Old Testament? The need for and interest in comparing Mesopotamian documents with the Old Testament has not abated, but it has been made more complex due to a number of factors. First, we have far more materials with which to work. Numerous copies and recensions of ancient documents, such as the *Gilgamesh Epic*, have been excavated. Whole libraries have been unearthed from ancient Mesopotamia and Syria—at Mari, Nuzi, Ebla, and Alalakh, for example—that were not available to Delitzsch or Gunkel. This body of documents is expanded when one considers inscriptions, ostraca, and papyri. We also have access to more linguistic reference works, such as *The Assyrian Dictionary*, originally organized by Ignace Gelb at the University of Chicago.

Another new factor is that we have access to numerous documents from ancient Ugarit (modern Ras Shamra) on the Syrian coast, discovered in 1928. Most of these documents are in Ugaritic, a Northwest Semitic language closely related to Hebrew and Aramaic. They provide material that is often much closer in terms of language, cultural references, and deities mentioned in the Old Testament. And as a port city, Ugarit was a genuine cultural crossroads, with documents not only in Ugaritic, but Akkadian, Sumerian, Egyptian, Hurrian, Hittite, and Cypro-Minoan as well.[4]

The comparative method itself has come a long way. Rather than speaking of relationships between documents from Babylon as "sources" of Old Testament materials, it is far better to speak of "parallels." That is, parallel lines may be close or far apart. But to say that two things are parallel is

4. See, for example, Cross, *Canaanite Myth and Hebrew Epic*; Fisher, editor, *Ras Shamra Parallels*, vols. 1–2; Rummel, editor, *Ras Shamra Parallels*, vol. 3; Brooke et al., editors, *Ugarit and the Bible*; Miller, "Aspects of Religion at Ugarit"; and Smith, *The Origins of Monotheism*.

often helpful even if we cannot trace the exact way in which they are related. Parallels may be observed at a variety of levels: linguistic (e.g., phonemes, phrases, formulas), cultural (e.g., marriage practices, governmental structures), or literary (e.g., plot, character, theme, motif), for instance. And each of those types of parallels manifests numerous subtypes.[5]

But comparisons are not the only relevant issues with regard to reading both the Old Testament and ancient Near Eastern documents. As Hallo points out, contrasts are also important to account for. He thus suggests a "contextual method" rather than a "comparative method." The context is both "horizontal" and "vertical":

> The "context" of a given text may be regarded as its horizontal dimension—the geographical, historical, religious, political and literary setting in which it was created and disseminated. The contextual approach tries to reconstruct and evaluate this setting, whether for a biblical text or one from the rest of the ancient Near East. Given the frequently very different settings of biblical and ancient Near Eastern texts, however, it is useful to recognize such contrasts as well as comparisons or, if one prefers, to operate with negative as well as positive comparison . . .
>
> But even where (positive) comparison is asserted, it is useful to raise questions of category and

5. See, for example, Evans et al., editors, *Essays on the Comparative Method*; Hallo et al., editors, *More Essays on the Comparative Method*; Younger et al., editors, *The Biblical Canon in Comparative Perspective*; Paden, "Comparison in the Study of Religion"; Walton, *Ancient Israelite Literature in Its Cultural Context*; and Walton, *Ancient Near Eastern Thought and the Old Testament*.

genre so that, as nearly as possible, like is compared with like . . .

But a text is not only the product of its contemporary context, its horizontal locus, as it were, in time and space. It also has its place on a vertical axis between the earlier texts that helped inspire it and the later texts that reacted to it. We can describe this feature of its interconnectedness as its vertical or, in line with current usage, its intertextual dimension.[6]

One of the things we have learned by having more documents; more knowledge of ancient Near Eastern languages, culture, and history; and more sophisticated tools with which to work is that some things that initially may have appeared to have a one-to-one correspondence (or something close to it) were actually common throughout the ancient Near East, or at least in multiple cultures. And historically, practices that were current in one era may have gone out of style for hundreds of years and then come back into practice again.

Why a New Edition?

Someone identified only as "E.S.B" produced the original translation of the present work. One might ask: "Why a revised translation and new edition?" I undertook revising the English edition because I find Gunkel's writing of enduring interest. His incisive mind, his broad-ranging knowledge of ancient literatures, and his attentiveness to the oral as well as the scribal in the history of tradition make him a genuine

---

6. Hallo, "Introduction," xxv–xxvi; and Hallo, "Compare and Contrast."

"great" in Old Testament studies. Because of my interest in him, I edited a volume of his essays as part of the series Fortress Classics in Biblical Studies, *Water for a Thirsty Land: Israelite Literature and Religion* (2001). And in recent years translations have finally appeared of *Genesis* (1977), *The Folktale in the Old Testament* (1987), *Introduction to the Psalms* (1998), and *Creation and Chaos* (2006).

Furthermore, the original translation was deficient in a number of respects,[7] especially:

- Phrases and sentences from the German original were inadvertently omitted altogether.

- The English syntax was sometimes allowed to mirror the German syntax, resulting in torturous or confusing sentences.

- The meanings of some German idioms were seriously misconstrued.

- The translator inserted his or her own views directly into the text so that it was not always immediately clear which comments were Gunkel's and which were those of the translator.

And finally, this volume makes Gunkel's critique available again. We reprinted Delitzsch's lectures in our Ancient Near East: Classic Studies series, and it seemed appropriate that we would make one of the most sustained critiques of those lectures available as well.

The reader should note that I have edited Gunkel's text in a number of ways:

---

7. This was pointed out by Carus in "Gunkel versus Delitzsch," 226–27. I will leave it to the reader to decide if I have done a better job.

- While the original German and first English editions both employed transliteration, I have added the Hebrew in parentheses.

- I have added numerous footnotes, preceded by [Ed.] to identify them as editorial. Notes added by the original translator are preceded by [E.S.B.].

- I have constructed a bibliography with three sections:

  » works Gunkel originally cited—both German and English editions are supplied whenever available;

  » works I cite in the Foreword and additional notes; and

  » works related to the Babel–Bible controversy.

- I have added three indexes:

  » ancient documents;

  » ancient personal names, divine names, and place names; and

  » modern authors.

- I have broken Gunkel's work into chapters and provided each with a title as well as adding a few headings.

- I have broken up long sentences and paragraphs.

- I have brought extensive content from Gunkel's notes into the body of the text, where it seemed to make better sense.

- I have used bullet lists in a few places where Gunkel originally had lists in paragraph form.

The original translator did us the favor of providing citations to Delitzsch's lectures both in their German original and in their English translation. The citation in the notes of "II:36–37 [207–8]," for example, refers to volume 2, pages 36–37 in the German, and pages 207–8 in the English translation. I have not preceded each with "Delitzsch."

Caveat lector

The one caveat I wish to make to the reader is that in several places Gunkel makes condescending or otherwise critical comments about modern Judaism that simply cannot be glossed over. I have made a few comments in the notes, but I did not feel it was necessary to flag every instance. This is an unfortunate aspect of Gunkel's attitude, and Susannah Heschel and others have documented what role this played in the church and biblical scholarship leading up to World War II.[8] It would also be unfair to think that only Germans have articulated such anti-Judaism. May it be a reminder to all of us that bigotry against those different from ourselves should not be countenanced.

---

8. Heschel, *Abraham Geiger and the Jewish Jesus*; Ericksen and Heschel, editors, *Betrayal*; Arnold and Weisberg, "A Centennial Review."

Abbreviations

ABD	*The Anchor Bible Dictionary*. 6 vols. Edited by David Noel Freedman. New York: Doubleday, 1992
AIR	*Ancient Israelite Religion: Essays in Honor of Frank Moore Cross*. Edited by Patrick D. Miller et al. Philadelphia: Fortress, 1987
ANECS	The Ancient Near East: Classic Studies
ANET	*Ancient Near Eastern Texts Relating to the Old Testament*. Edited by James B. Pritchard. 3rd ed. Princeton: Princeton University Press, 1969
AnOr	Analecta Orientalia
ATT	Ancient Texts and Translations
COS	*The Context of Scripture*. 3 vols. Edited by William W. Hallo. Leiden: Brill, 1997, 2000, 2002
CH	Code of Hammurabi
DDD	*Dictionary of Deities and Demons in the Bible*. Edited by Karel van der Toorn et al. 2nd ed. Leiden: Brill, 1999
TDOT	*Theological Dictionary of the Old Testament*. 15 vols. Edited by G. Johannes Botterweck, Helmer Ringgren, and Heinz-Josef Fabry. Translated by John T. Willis and David E. Green. Grand Rapids: Eerdmans, 1974–

1

Delitzsch, Babylon, and the Bible

For the past year the German public has been in an uproar over the topic of "Babel and Bible." How does one explain the sensation that Delitzsch's lectures have elicited? This is a question that certainly demands consideration. In the first place, the initial lecture, which created the stir among the public, offers scarcely anything in terms of research material beyond what has already been known by all Assyriologists and students of Old Testament theology as well—something that is granted on all sides. In other words, the lecture was, and evidently claimed to be, only a fuller and more lucid review of contemporary results.

In order to explain the sensation that arose so suddenly, it is necessary to remember the conditions under which our journalists operate. The daily press lives from day to day on "events" under its own conditions. Any development that proceeds slowly easily escapes notice. But if a sudden and fortuitous occurrence brings matters to the surface, then the event suddenly becomes "news" and remains so until something else more "newsworthy" overtakes it. And so it happened that our newspapers had taken little notice of the quiet but expanding research in Assyriology, in much the same way as they ignore academic theology in general (despite the few noteworthy exceptions lately). Whatever can be read in the daily papers on such issues (and especially on Old Testament subjects) is usually of negligible research value. And this is not excused by the fact that many educated persons, including those of the highest circles—even many university teachers (as is evident from time to time) with whom we teach daily and in adjacent rooms—that even such as these know nothing of the existence of serious academic theology, have no conceptions of the method of our work, and are ignorant of the results of that work, despite all our endeavors to popularize them.

And with this complete ignorance of research relating to religion, *dilettantism* is in full bloom as it is scarce elsewhere. Many hold opinions regarding religion without being able to join in a conversation on the least technical topic. What we experience anew each day in this regard is horrifying, really horrifying! So one can observe how even researchers, who in their own domain are quite sober and temperate, suddenly lose their balance when they discuss religion. And now research on Babylonian–Biblical topics has suddenly become "news," as if a light-bearer from above had suddenly flooded it with a stream of light. The entire world devoured this lecture, which the highest person in our country twice had delivered before him.[1]

1. [Ed.] This refers to Delitzsch's invitation to give his lectures before Kaiser Wilhelm II, emperor of Germany and king of Prussia, and the Deutsche Orient-Gesellschaft.

But as little as the public had previously understood of these things the more it has now been astonished to see an entire buried world rise here in the light of day. Unfortunately, Delitzsch had neglected to state in the text of his lecture in completely unequivocal terms that the material compiled by him is substantially—and especially in so far as it is assured—a common possession of an entire generation of research. A segment of the public—and perhaps no small segment—has consequently misunderstood him entirely, and regards his lecture as a most remarkable scientific achievement.

At the same time, ecclesiastical circles have become violently agitated. Delitzsch has recognized the results of modern Old Testament research. For instance, he designated as a scientifically unassailable and enduring fact the assertion that the Pentateuch has been composed of very distinct literary sources. He certainly asserted a primitive Babylonian origin for some of the most familiar portions of Israel's traditions—particularly the narratives of creation, the flood, and paradise—and accordingly declared himself of the opinion that these stories are to be regarded as myths and legends, not as objective descriptions of real events. Moreover, the Sabbath is of Babylonian origin, and an analogy is to be found there for monotheism itself.

Yet with all these assertions Delitzsch did not say much more than is generally admitted among scholars, or is, at least, under discussion. In spite of that, his words affected many in the community like a thunderbolt. Many things may come into consideration to explain so unexpected a result. But the principal cause is, after all, the lamentable estrangement of the Protestant Church from Protestant research. The origin of this estrangement and the source of blame for it need not be discussed here; only the fact itself is unfortunately

Ishtar Gate of Babylon

indisputable. How few among the educated persons of the community, even among the older clergy—and not only among the *older* clergy—have a clear conception of what is actually going on currently in academic theology? It is this that makes it possible for these "Bible–Babylonian" investigations, when once they have become news, to surprise the Church and catch it quite defenseless.

Now had the Church employed a prudent and vigorous theology, it could have indicated which aspects of Delitzsch's assertions were correct and which somewhat exaggerated. But even if many cautious words *were* spoken, nonetheless the voices of the excited participants rose much louder. The one side called out: The Bible is disposed of, once and for all. Assyriology has proved that its entire substance is Babylonian! And the other fought with the energy of desperation to recognize only a tittle of Israel's religion as adopted from foreign sources. And between these two extremes a bewildering multitude of opinions, reflecting back the complete chaos of our troubled age in a myriad of forms. Even the Jewish community rose up in fright at losing its reputation as the chosen people if Israel's traditions were of Babylonian origin. Personal quarrels (which perhaps were better avoided) were added to the mix. On more or less prominent sides, a deluge of articles appeared in newspapers and journals, lectures with and without illustrations, and brochures of every description. Clarifications or other publications in the newspapers repeatedly goaded the discussions anew. This resulted in a colossal confusion.

But this confusion has been further increased by Delitzsch's recently delivered second lecture. To be sure, as far as regards substance, this lecture also brought nothing special to the expert. But now the Assyriologist, irritated by his ecclesiastical opponents, proceeded into the theological realm and summarily placed in question the revelatory character of the Old Testament and the religion of Israel itself.

But on the same day this lecture was delivered, the public was astonished by another great sensation: a letter from the emperor destroyed the widespread error that Delitzsch's principal assertions were accompanied in all respects by the very highest approval. So the attention of the widest circles was drawn again to this discussion, and the flood of publications began once more. And now a third lecture is to be expected, concerning which we read here and there mysterious hints.

So the author of these lines has likewise felt it his duty not to refuse the many appeals that have come to him, and for his part to assist in helping to quiet the growing confusion. Many considerations might certainly have inclined him rather to silence than to speech, for scientific research seeks quiet and abhors sensation. And as difficult as it may be for the investigator that no one notices his painstaking work, it is dangerous when the uproar of the day rages about him and may drown out what is best in him—the pure and judicious intention that is needful to him above everything. Let us say then, once and for all, in all honesty and truth: favor to none and malice toward none! The author may assume that many readers will be astonished or amazed by some or other of his words, although he plans in general not to go beyond what he can assume to be the general conviction of his colleagues. But he also begs the readers, if they are of a different opinion in many things, at least to *believe* that he seeks the truth with all his might, and that in expressing it to a larger circle he has no wish but to serve our beloved Protestant Church.

2

The Broad Reach of Babylonian Civilization

Let us begin with a few words on Babylonian civilization in general. The decipherment of the cuneiform inscriptions is one of the most brilliant achievements of the human intellect. Since that time our view of the ancient Near East has altered completely. While the scholars of earlier generations were bound to the scanty reports in the Old Testament and by the Greeks regarding the ancient Near East, we now know it from indigenous sources, and these sources begin, at the latest, about 3000 BCE! The history of our species has been extended two full millennia right before our eyes! What a powerful scientific event! And how multicolored a historical picture it is that rolls out in front of us, fragmentary though it may be for the present! Peoples appear, flourish, and disappear! Tremendous, worldwide conquering empires arise and struggle for supremacy.

But the center of the ancient Near East is Babylonia—there, from inconceivable ages past, an amazingly high culture reigned, which is found already in full bloom circa

3000 BCE. This culture derives from a non-Semitic people, called Sumerians, and is then taken up and carried further by Semitic immigrants. And this culture was carried forth from Babylonia throughout the entire ancient Near East as far as Egypt. In the ancient Near East, Babylon takes the position that Rome occupied thousands of years later in the West. This Babylonian world-civilization we see operating down to Greco-Roman times; in fact, its last traces we have in our very midst. A few particulars here must suffice to make clear the immeasurable importance of the Babylonian culture.

Recently the scholarly world has been surprised by the discovery of the law book of the Babylonian king Hammurabi, dated about 2250 BCE.[1] This law book reveals to us complex social relations and a code embodying finely developed laws, which, in part, were far more civilized than those of Israel in the so-called Mosaic law.[2] For instance, in Babylon the law of blood-revenge had disappeared, while it still ruled in ancient Israel. Or, to name just one other point that demonstrates the height of Babylonian civilization, the Hammurabi Code contains regulations for physicians' fees! And this law was codified about 2250 BCE; it stems from a period a thousand years before Israel existed. It is as far removed from Moses as we are from Charlemagne!

In order to illustrate the wide extent of the Babylonian influence, let us mention another discovery that threw a sudden light on these things a few years ago (1887)—the discovery of

1. [Ed.] The dating of Hammurabi is uncertain. The high, middle, and low chronologies of the beginning of his reign are 1848, 1792, or 1736 BCE (based on astrological data); see Meier, "Hammurapi," 40.

2. [Ed.] For translation, see Roth, "The Laws of Hammurabi"; and Richardson, *Hammurabi's Laws*.

Tell Amarna in Egypt.[3] The archives of Amenophis IV were excavated there, and in them was revealed the correspondence of the Pharaohs with the kings in Babylonia, Assyria, Mesopotamia, Cyprus, as well as with the Egyptian vassals in Canaan. From this international correspondence, which was carried on in the Babylonian language, it was seen that Babylonian was then the international diplomatic language of the entire ancient Near East. The petty kings of Canaan themselves, who lived under Egyptian suzerainty, wrote to their Egyptian lord, not on Egyptian material (papyrus) or in the Egyptian language, but on Babylonian material (clay tablets) and in the Babylonian language!

Amarna tablets

3. [Ed.] For an introduction to and translation of the Amarna letters, see Moran, *Amarna Letters*.

Let us consider what the dominance of a foreign language in diplomatic communications must mean for the entire civilization. Syria and Canaan must have been subject at that time to the influence of Babylonian culture, in much the same way, perhaps, as in the eighteenth century the whole educated world—and therefore the diplomats as well—spoke French! This correspondence, however, which displays an extension of the Babylonian civilization as far as Canaan, dates from the period 1500–1400 BCE. Canaan was, with regard to its culture, a Babylonian province, before Israel invaded it.

Another image: In later times, when Persians, Greeks, and Romans mingled, when religions became intertwined and new composite concepts arose, the Babylonian element is still visible. We hear repeatedly during this period of seven highest *genii* or deities—these are the seven Babylonian planet-deities. These are the same forms (to assume this here in advance) that continue in the Judeo-Christian tradition as the seven highest angels—the seven archangels. In the various speculations, which streamed in from the ancient Near East during the first Christian centuries, and even gained a foothold in some Christian circles—speculations which we choose to term "Gnostic"—in these, there still re-echo traces of the (partly) primitive Babylonian mythology.

Yes, even among us there are a few things that recall Babylonian wisdom, although of course only faintly. The Babylonians became the teachers of our whole world civilization, especially in astronomy and in all branches dependent on it—mathematics and measurement. We still divide the zodiac into twelve signs and the circle into 360 degrees. And modern Christians still call the seven days of the week after the seven planet-deities of the Babylonians: Sunday [Šamaš], Monday [Sîn], Tuesday [French, *Mardi*, Ninib or Käîvânu],

Wednesday [French, *Mercredi*, Nabû], Thursday [Marduk], Friday [Ištar], Saturday [Nergal].[4] These names were taken over by the modern world from Graeco-Roman civilization, but the latter obtained them from the ancient Near East—originally from Babylonia.

It is understandable that modern investigators would become ecstatic when they contemplate such a tremendous history. And every day may bring new discoveries, for we certainly are not yet at the end of these investigations. There are still whole libraries of clay tablets beneath the ground awaiting the fortunate discoverer, and even of those already found only a portion have been read and evaluated.[5] So we understand how Assyriology reaches out on all sides in an ecstasy of youthful and ardent exuberance, how it investigates Greek culture, Roman law, and the religion of Israel from a Babylonian perspective. That the older fields of research resist such "Babylonizing" attempts is understandable enough. Greek scholars, for example, will not soon be able to admit much that, until now, they have regarded as indigenously Hellenic as imported from the ancient Near East.

But in spite of all opposition, we may safely assume that such investigations will come in the future, as far as they have not come already, and will bear fruit for research.[6] On

---

4. [E.S.B.] The names of the deities were not in the original German. Note Käivânu and Nergal were later interchanged.

5. [Ed.] How prophetic Gunkel was here. He wrote before the great discoveries of tablets from Nuzi, Ugarit, and Ebla or the manuscript discoveries from Qumran and Nag Hammadi.

6. [Ed.] See my Web page "Parallels and Connections between the Hellenic, Semitic, and Anatolian Cultures" for a classified bibliography on relations between the Hellenic world and the ancient Near East. See also Burkert, *The Orientalizing Revolution*.

the other hand also it is to be borne in mind that trees do not grow up to the heavens. The result will assuredly not be that the whole world is Babylonian at its foundation. The Babylonian influence may have been considerable—perhaps even more considerable than we can suspect at this time. And yet even now it may be safely stated that the great peoples of antiquity who came later than the Babylonians and on whose foundation our intellectual culture is built—especially Israel, Hellas, and Rome—each has its own characteristic individuality. And this is despite the occasional and perhaps deep Babylonian influence.

3

Babylonian Influences and Delitzsch's Misinterpretations

And so we come to our main theme: *What influence did the Babylonian world have on Israel, especially on Israelite religion?*

But with this we enter a realm where the Old Testament theologian has a full right to enter the discussion as a specialist, while until now he could simply report. It is necessary to state this explicitly. For some Assyriologists—we say with regret—have assumed a proprietary tone towards the older field of Old Testament studies, as if the only legitimate way to understand Israel from now on proceeds through Assyriology, and as if in Old Testament research Assyriology could dispense with the collaboration of the theologian.

Neither has Delitzsch kept himself entirely free from this tone—in spite of the words of high appreciation that he first expressed for our field[1]—in the later stages of the debate,

1. I:4 [4].

when he was certainly quite irritated by uninformed opponents (and this should not be overlooked). One can only read with mixed feelings Delitzsch's comment that he expects from the Babylonian monuments ("which our expedition will set to work to excavate") a more notable and rapid advance in the linguistic understanding of the Old Testament than has been possible for two thousand years.[2] No one can be blamed for thinking highly of his own field of research; and even if he overestimates its value, such human weakness will readily be pardoned. But, at the same time, one must not ask too much patience of his neighbor. The one who sets off for battle is not esteemed the same as the one who returns home.[3]

But, in reality, the situation is that Assyriology already encompasses an almost immeasurable domain. And, on the other hand, Old Testament research lays claim to the complete powers of an ordinary mortal, so that only to a genius for whom there are no such restrictions would it be possible really to unite both fields. We Old Testament theologians are accordingly admonished to learn from the Assyriologist when he instructs us in Babylonian matters, and also when he explains the Hebrew linguistic usages on the basis of Babylonian. But, on the other hand, we have the right to insist that the Assyriologist likewise remain within the boundaries of his own field.

The Assyriologist who in any way compares Israelite matters with Babylonian and seeks to draw a conclusion from the comparison places himself in a realm where he is not ordinarily an expert in the full sense of the word. *And he*

2. II:14 [167–68].

3. [Ed.] I take this as a German proverb or popular saying, which Gunkel uses metaphorically here.

should bear that in mind. Even "Hebrew philology" provides no real inner understanding of the religion of Israel. So both subjects are in a friendly relation, appropriate for collaboration. We wish wholeheartedly that both fields might reach out to one another afresh for the common task, where each honors the other and strives to learn from the other. May the Assyriologist who wishes to speak on Old Testament issues call the theologian into consultation if he does not feel himself completely competent on this subject!

So Delitzsch, whom we highly esteem as an Assyriologist and Hebrew philologian, would have done well, perhaps, if he had employed the advice of some expert and prudent specialist on the Old Testament before he offered his opinions on Old Testament religion to the general public. Perhaps the Old Testament scholar would have pointed out to him at the appropriate time where some linguistic oversight had escaped him,[4] or where he had even failed to consult the original text.

Delitzsch cites *loʾ liqṭol* (לֹא לִקְטֹל) "You shall not kill"; as a matter of fact, both places (Exod 20:13; Deut 5:17) read *loʾ tirṣaḥ* (לֹא תִרְצַח), "You shall not commit murder."[5] "We scholars would count it a grave reproach to anyone of ourselves to render falsely or inaccurately . . . even in a single letter, the inscription of anyone."[6] The Old Testament colleague would not have allowed hazardous opinions concerning the interpretations of many biblical passages to escape his notice, or otherwise would have pointed out incorrect or dubious

---

4. Delitzsch refers (in I:38, 39 [57]) to *dem Scheol* [masculine, an error lost in the English]; the word is feminine.

5. II:26 [188].

6. II:21 [180]. [Ed.] The unfortunate awkwardness of this quotation is from the published English translation.

assertions of all sorts. He would have taken pains to explain our religio-historical understanding of the Old Testament, and he would have warned him against entering into questions of systematic theology.

Delitzsch is completely wrong when discussing the well-known passage of Genesis 1:27: "So God created man in his own image, in the image of God he created him; male and female he created them." He thinks this possibly has a polytheistic coloring, distinguishing gods and goddesses.[7] This was certainly not the thought of the rigidly monotheistic writer of Genesis 1; and, just as little, there is no ground whatsoever to regard this polytheistic coloring as the original thought in the material. Rather it means simply: (1) the human is created in the image of God; (2) when the humans were created, they were male and female.

How Delitzsch can find in Job 24:18–19 the later Jewish concept of the twofold recompense in the underworld is incomprehensible to me.[8]

From Isaiah 66:24 ("their worm shall not die, neither shall their fire be quenched"), Delitzsch deduces that cremation is thought of in the Old Testament as standing entirely on the same level with inhumation; and the deduction is coupled with a wearying reference to modern times. He concludes from this passage that there is not the slightest opposition to cremation from the biblical side.[9] But his conception of the passage is wrong; for it is quite well known to us that the ordinary, honorable form in ancient Israel was burial, while the burning of the body was regarded as a horrifying shame.

7. I:64 [106].
8. I:39 [59]; [Ed.] See also [I:118–19].
9. I:69 [120].

Isaiah 66:24 contains, however, no reference to the ordinary disposition of the body, but is speaking of the horrible fate of the apostates, who, met by the judgment of God, lay dead *on the fields*, decaying or disposed of by burning.

Likewise the translation of Habakkuk 3:4, "horns at his side,"[10] is off base. The parallelism with *nôgah* (נֹגַהּ), "brightness," and the context ("and there was the hiding of his power"), shows rather that the word should be translated "rays." Accordingly, Delitzsch's opinion that Israel, as well as the Babylonians, had conceived of their deity as horned collapses entirely.

The assertion that the song of Jonah (2:2–9) is a mosaic of Psalm passages is,[11] in my opinion, as wrong as considering Psalm 45 as a mere "love song."[12] At least Delitzsch should have expressed these views with some limitations. The remark that today "we" are still looking for Mount Sinai in the range of the Sinai Peninsula[13] is not true with any such generality. In fact, many modern writers believe that it could not have been situated there. Here as well Delitzsch proves himself not to have sufficiently mastered the facts.

Delitzsch's polemic against modern textual criticism of the Old Testament is without merit.[14] Of course the rich Assyrian lexicon is of the utmost importance for Hebrew, which often is deficient. And it is likewise possible to explain many passages, which have been given up on by our field or which we could hope to reach only through textual emendations,

10. II:31 [196].
11. II:16 [171].
12. II:19 [176].
13. II:22 [181].
14. II:14 [166].

by means of reference to the Babylonian. But by such means the assured knowledge of these generations of scholars is in no way invalidated, namely, that many passages of the Old Testament are corrupt beyond recovery.

The etymological explanation of "Yahweh" as "the One Who Exists" is as dubious as that of "El" (God) as "Goal."[15] Delitzsch should not have made such declarations without great reserve. He has done so for "Yahweh,"[16] but he has neglected to do so for "El."[17]

In many places it is evident that Delitzsch possesses no proper *historical* understanding of the Old Testament; this would be no reproach for an Assyriologist who sticks to his own subject. This is seen most strongly when Delitzsch names the God who appears to Moses amid thunder and earthquake: "The All-enfolding, The All-upholding."[18] Delitzsch treats the conception of the God of Moses and that of Faust as the same!

Another remarkable error against exegesis, as taught by the history of religion, is the translation of Genesis 12:8, where Abram is supposed to have "preached" in the name of Yahweh.[19] *Preached!* Preached to whom? Certainly not to the Canaanites! The word in question [קרא, *qrʾ*] means in

---

15. [Ed.] See Pope, *El in the Ugaritic Texts*; Cross, "*Canaanite Myth and Hebrew Epic*, 44–75; Cross, "אל *El*"; Freedman and O'Conner, "יהוה *YHWH*"; Herrmann, "El"; and van der Toorn, "Yahweh."

16. I:47 [71].

17. I:45 [69].

18. II:21 [179]. [E.S.B.] Goethe's *Faust*, pt. I, sc. 16; Taylor's translation.

19. II:29 [193].

that passage, as all moderns will agree, not "to preach" but "to invoke," as in ancient worship.[20]

Since Moses, in his anger, smashed the tables written by the hand of God, he will have to bear a reproach, so thinks Delitzsch, ascending in a unanimous cry from all peoples of the earth.[21] The viewpoint of the old folktale is so much loftier, when represents the hero's anger at Israel's sin as so great that he threw the divine tablets to the ground in blinding anger. What would Michelangelo have said if he had known of this prosaic remark by Delitzsch!

In Delitzsch's opinion, some words in the book of Job border on blasphemy and so exclude the Old Testament from being a book of revelation.[22] How much greater and freer were the creators of the canon when they included Job in the Scriptures, in spite of the *apparent* blasphemies! For what sort of blasphemies are they? The mightiest outpouring of a heroic man, who fears to lose his God, the stability of his life, who fights for God and justice with tears of desperation in his eyes!

Delitzsch concludes that the fifth, sixth, and seventh commandments owe their origin to the instinct of self-preservation.[23] Really, now, *only* to that instinct? The national laws of Israel were, "with a view to enhancing their sacred character and inviolability, [referred back] to Yahweh himself, as the supreme Lawgiver."[24] Delitzsch here, quite in the manner of the older rationalism, understands [the origin of these

20. [Ed.] See Gunkel, *Genesis*, 167.
21. II:21 [179].
22. II:19 [176].
23. II:28 [190–91].
24. II:23 [184].

commandments] as consciously intentional, when in reality they originated as unintentional, naïve, self-understood. The ancient codes of this very ancient people, he is convinced, were not created by the living generation, nor by their ancestors, nor by men at all; they are far too wise and wonderful for such a source; the Deity himself provided them. This assertion has an entirely different origin when it is made not of laws that are a national inheritance, as was the case in Israel, but of a recently formed code; the latter is true of Hammurabi.

It is likewise unhistorical when Delitzsch considers the idea of original revelation as discredited by a single verse of the Old Testament.[25] But is the Old Testament a system in which there can be no contradiction, or does it not rather contain a varied plenitude of records of a great religio-historical process in which there have actually been all sorts of different positions? In this case if a single verse is to exclude an original revelation, why should another not contain this idea?

Delitzsch charges the collection of short pieces [*Flugschriften*] included in the book of Daniel with "mistakes and inaccuracies."[26] But the legends in this book are *folk traditions*, which we have no right to measure by the standard of strict history.

As an example of the *frivolity* with which people have handled the Ten Commandments, Delitzsch also brings up the division of the Commandments that is customary in the Lutheran Church.[27] Regarding the matter itself, Delitzsch is unquestionably right. But who would adduce such a trifle to prove that humanity has not served a further divine revela-

25. II:3, 37 [151, 207]. [Ed.] Delitzsch refers to Deut 4:19.
26. II:16 [170].
27. II:20 [178].

tion? Why not allow a modern church to arrange the ancient material in its own way for practical purposes?

That different generations may have a different understanding of the sacred story—which is self-evident in the historical sense—is something Delitzsch cannot bring himself to see. In ancient exposition such as Hebrews 1:8–9, he sees only aberrations.[28] He even finds fault that the expression "where their worm never dies" stands in Jesus's description of hellfire (Mark 9:44, 46, 48).[29] Thus Delitzsch parades our, or his, *modern* conception [of the afterlife] as obvious and demands even of the New Testament era that it follow this explanation! *Moreover, does Delitzsch not use a critical edition of the New Testament?* Had he consulted a modern critical edition, he would have noticed that Mark 9:44, 46, which he cites along with v. 48, are currently regarded as spurious, and that since only the last clause of v. 43 (possibly with that of v. 45), but not that of vv. 47ff., speak of hell *fire*, his whole observation fails.[30] But what would Delitzsch say about a theologian who dealt so uncritically with Assyriological matters? *And why does Delitzsch discuss the New Testament in which he is manifestly not at home?*

The manner in which he explains the meaning of El ("God"), which according to him means "Goal," is also quite unhistorical. The Deity is the Goal, that is "the Being to whom as to a goal the eyes of man looking heavenwards are turned, 'on whom hangs the gaze of every man, to whom man looks out from afar' (Job xxxvi.25), that Being towards whom

28. II:19 [177].

29. I:69 [120].

30. [Ed.] Metzger, *A Textual Commentary on the Greek New Testament*, ad loc.

man stretches forth his hands, after whom the human heart yearns away from the mutability and imperfection of earthly life"![31] What a crass modernization! As if it were *self-evident* to a "*human*" that he seeks the Deity in heaven, and that he yearns after him from the mutability of this world!

It is unhistorical as well when Delitzsch asserts that Genesis 1 does not contain the idea that God is the Almighty Creator of heaven and earth because it leaves the question unanswered: "Whence did chaos originate?"[32] But the idea of "creation" has its *history*; therefore we can properly say that this idea in Genesis 1 concerning chaos was not *thought through* to its ultimate conclusion. But we cannot doubt that the priestly author of this section would have wished to express this idea. Yet we dare not seek such finer distinctions in Delitzsch.

According to Deuteronomy 4:19—which, incidentally, is well known to Old Testament scholars as a matter of course, although Delitzsch calls it "forgotten"[33]—God has assigned the host of heaven (viz. the stars) to the various peoples. Delitzsch completely misunderstands the passage if he thinks that God himself has abandoned all the heathens to godlessness.[34] The meaning is rather that the stars are actually divine beings, even if subordinate to Yahweh. Furthermore, it shows a total lack of method when Delitzsch combines this verse with Deuteronomy 7:2, according to which Yahweh commands Israel to exterminate the peoples of Canaan, and when he calls it a "dreadful" thought, that Yahweh should so

31. I:45–46 [69–70].
32. I:65 [109].
33. II:3 [151].
34. II:36–37 [207–8].

mercilessly punish the peoples, whom he himself has abandoned to godlessness—and *because* he has so abandoned
them. In this manner Delitzsch combines passages that have
no inner-connection; he handles Deuteronomy as though it
were admittedly the work of a single author. This is a method
that we would not tolerate in those doing research under us.
But that the two passages have no inner-connection is clear.
In no sense does Deuteronomy 7:2 presuppose that the idol-
worship of the Canaanites is from Yahweh. Moreover, the
point here is not that Yahweh wishes to destroy the people of
Canaan "*on account of their godlessness*," but rather lest they
seduce Israel to idolatry.

If Delitzsch had followed all this advice, the first lecture
would have taken a different form in many respects, and the
second would not have been delivered at all, to the benefit
both of the subject and assuredly of Delitzsch!

4

Babylonian Influences on Israelite Culture

Let us for the moment leave religion out of the question and ask: *May we assume an influence of Babylon on Israel's culture?* To this question we may with complete certainty answer yes. The influence is evident and must in fact have been enormous.

In Israel there were, above all, Babylonian systems of measure, weight, and coinage. Babylonian was the striking preference of Israelite culture—even of the literature—for particular numbers (e.g., 7 and 12), a preference that in Babylonia is explained by the fact that particular numbers are characteristic of particular astral deities. And Israel's tendency to group literary creations according to these numbers has been proved for Babylon: the great Babylonian creation epic was written on seven tables,[1] and the national epic of *Gilgamesh* on twelve.[2]

1. [Ed.]*Enuma elish*; for the text, see Foster, *Before the Muses*, 436–86; Foster, "Epic of Creation"; Dalley, *Myths from Mesopotamia*, 228–77.

2. [Ed.] For the text of the *Gilgamesh Epic*, see George, *The Epic of Gilgamesh*; and Dalley, *Myths from Mesopotamia*, 39–153; for analysis,

The Code of Hammurabi has delivered new surprises:[3]

- The Babylonian also followed the precept: "An eye for eye and tooth for tooth" (CH §§196, 198, 200; Exod 21:24–25).

- Like the Israelite, he performed the ceremony of adoption by pronouncing the words: "You are my son" (CH §§170–171; Ps 2:7); and he denied his subjection to another by saying: "You are not my father or my lord" (CH §§192, 282; Hosea 1–2).

- When Laban and Jacob negotiated with each other, the legal basis of their compact was Babylonian law: in a case involving the death of a sheep by wild beasts, the damage is borne by the owner (CH §§244, 266; Gen 31:39).

- And the one who accuses another of theft has the right to institute a search of the other's house before witnesses (CH §9).

- The same is true in the case of barrenness: the Babylonian married woman, like the ancient Hebrew woman, can give her husband a maid so that she may raise up children (CH §144; Genesis 16). The story of Hagar the slave, who became a mother in this way and exalted herself over her mistress (Genesis 16),[4] is a parade example of Babylonian law (CH §146).

---

see Tigay, *The Evolution of the Gilgamesh Epic*.

3. [Ed.] For the text of the Code of Hammurabi, see Richardson, *Hammurabi's Laws*; and Roth, "The Laws of Hammurabi."

4. [Ed.] For further analysis, see Gunkel, "The Hagar Traditions"; and Gunkel, *Genesis*, 183–92.

But enough of details! We see sufficiently from these few examples
that Israel did not remain free from
Babylonian influence.

In the same way, we can mention the periods in which Babylonia especially affected Israel. The
most important is the period of
the height of the Assyrian empire,
about 660 BCE, when the Babylonian gods, as gods of the Assyrian
realm, were esteemed in the entire
ancient Near Eastern world as the
mightiest deities. That is the period
when even Egyptian cities bore of-
ficial Babylonian names and when
the Babylonian gods were revered
by the state of Judah.[5] Their em-
blems and altars stood in Yahweh's
temple on Zion at that time. And

Hammurabi Stele

the Judeans again came under Babylonian influence when
Nebuchadnezzar deported all "the officers and the mighty of
the land" to Babylonia (2 Kgs 24:15), and so brought them
into the immediate sphere of Babylon. Postexilic Judaism was
completely subjugated by the influence of this world culture
in all domains of external life. In the centuries following the
exile, the people had actually forgotten their native language
and adopted the Aramaic language, which then dominated

5. [Ed.] See van der Toorn et al., editors, *Dictionary of Deities and
Demons in the Old Testament*; Miller, *The Religion of Ancient Israel*; and
Smith, *The Origins of Biblical Monotheism*.

the entire Semitic cultural world. It had finally become, in this way, a completely different people, who were bound to the ancient Israelite people by only a slender thread.

But much weightier than deductions from these later eras is a fact that we know from the Tell Amarna letters, namely, that Canaan was already most thoroughly permeated by Babylonian influence before the settlement of Israel. Accordingly, when Israel entered Canaan and soaked in ancient Canaanite culture, it came indirectly under the dominion of Babylonian civilization. It is no surprise to us, therefore, if the oldest stories—such as those just mentioned about Jacob and Laban, and Hagar and Sarah—presuppose Babylonian legal conditions.

And this influence never completely ceased, for Israel's territory lay on the great commercial roads, which led from Babylonia to Egypt. Merchants traveled on these great international roads with their goods; the conquerors with their armies; but also ideas, myths, legends, and religions. And that the Babylonian religion traveled in this way to Canaan is not simply assumption but something that we can confirm by examples: Mt. Sinai is probably named after the Babylonian moon-god Sîn;[6] and Mount Nebo, where Moses died, is named after the Babylonian Nebô.[7]

On the other hand, it would certainly be very perverse if we described Israel as *nothing more* than a Babylonian province. With its primevally ancient civilization that rivaled the Babylonian, Egypt surely lay much too near for it not to

6. [Ed.] For this and other possibilities, see Maiberger and Dohmen, "סיני *sinay*," 218–20.

7. [Ed.] The Babylonian deity's name is now commonly written Nabû; Gunkel's identification is disputed by Millard, "Nabû," 609.

have had a similar effect. Egyptian policy had indeed, at various times, reckoned Canaan and Syria as part of its own sphere of influence. One need only recall the role that Egypt and Egyptian life played in the story of Joseph to recognize how much ancient Israel had concerned itself with Egypt. But that the Hebrews, together with the allied Phoenicians and Arameans, had something of their *own* in their culture is evidenced most clearly by the fact that they possessed their *own writing*; they wrote in neither Egyptian nor Babylonian.[8] And it is well known that tendencies towards affinity reveal themselves in all civilizations most clearly in their writing. Accordingly, one must guard here as well from exaggeration.

Babylonian god Nabu

8. [Ed.] See Peckham, "Phoenicia and the Religion of Israel"; and Greenfield, "Aspects of Aramean Religion."

5

Babylonian Influences on Israelite Religion

Let us now ask: *Does Israel's religion also manifest Babylonian traces?* That the historian has the right—yes, even the duty—to open this question, can, after the preceding, surely not be in doubt. But may theology as such, may we as Christians, who believe in the revelation of God in the religion of Israel, take part in such undertakings? Is not faith in God's revelation brought down if we find Babylonian elements in this religion? Delitzsch's orthodox opponents have answered these questions affirmatively and have fought with all their might against the assumption of Babylonian elements in the Bible. But the extremists on the other side are of the same opinion as well, and for just that reason are rejoicing over the downfall of the Bible and religion.

What then is our position to be as opposed to this? A faith—we must say—that is worthy of the name must be *courageous* and *bold*. What kind of a faith would it be that is afraid of facts, which abhors scholarly research? If we really believe in

God, who reveals himself in history, then we are not to dictate to the Almighty in what events we should find him; rather we only have to kiss his feet humbly and honor his rule in history. If we have to alter our views of God's ways in history because the facts teach us—well, we simply have to do so!

If, therefore, we really find Babylonian elements in the religion of Israel, yes, even if they were absolutely important and weighty matters, yet our faith should nevertheless *rejoice* that the world is opening itself to us and that we see God's rule where we formerly had not suspected it. Judaism, in which matters religious and national are always closely related, may be anxious lest a pearl be stolen from its crown. But what are the national claims of Judaism to us? We cheerfully and honestly acknowledge God's revelation wherever a human soul feels itself near its God, even though that be in the most arid and peculiar forms. Far be it from us to limit God's revelation to Israel! "The seed is sown on the whole wide land!" How much more nobly than the modern "orthodox" have the Fathers of the Christian Church thought, who in the great and noble heroes of Greek philosophy have seen bearers of the seed of the divine Word, seed sown everywhere. Let us Christians not likewise commit the incivility of Judaism, which thinks to honor its God by despising and abusing all other religions.[1] To use an image from the Bible, the Israelite-Christian religion is the firstborn among its brothers. We truly have no need to defend our own territory jealously; we ought to be sufficiently open-minded to recognize—and even among those ancient Babylonians—what there is to

---

1. [Ed.] This unfortunate slur cannot be sustained against Judaism in general, and it is certainly true of members of almost all religious groups.

recognize. The height and majesty of Israel's religion will not thereby be lessened, but for the first time be placed properly in the light.

But in any case, be that as it may, we are resolved to hear the facts—not to resist them inwardly, but to submit to them willingly. And therein lies our honor as researchers.

In the first lecture, Delitzsch listed a series of points in which the Babylonian religion has supposedly influenced that of Israel; these are in the first place biblical narratives—the flood, the creation, and paradise. These are supposedly stem from Babylonian tradition. How does the case stand?

Flood Narratives

The story of the flood is unquestionably of Babylonian origin.[2] Almost all modern scholars—Assyriologists and Old Testament scholars—agree in this. And if isolated, overly anxious theologians struggle against this indisputable conclusion, they may well consider whether they are not doing more harm than good to the cause of the faith they defend. Alas for theology and alas for our church as well, if it takes closing its eyes to obvious facts as its calling!

The situation is as follows: The Babylonians also have a story of the flood whose whole design coincides in a remarkable manner with both the biblical accounts—*both*, for there are *two* stories of the flood in Genesis that have been edited together by a third hand.[3] The weightiness of the subject

2. A more complete discussion of the Babylonian-Israelite relations in the legend will be found in Gunkel, "Babylonische und biblische Urgeschichte." [Ed.] See also Gunkel, *Genesis*, 60–79, 138–51.

3. [Ed.] Gunkel refers here to the accounts of the Yahwist (J) and the Priestly writers (P), edited by the priestly redactor (R^P). For a visual

requires that we pause here a bit longer. The Babylonian story, which has come down to us in a wonderfully poetic form, tells how the gods decided to destroy the city of Šuruppak (probably situated at the mouth of the Euphrates).[4] But Ea, the god of wisdom, wished to save his favorite, Ut-Napištim, who was equal to his patron god in wisdom. But since Ea did not dare disclose the counsel of the great gods to a human, he adopted a stratagem: he appeared to the human at night, while he was sleeping by the wall of his reed-house, and commanded the *house*, the *wall*, to build a ship! But the human, wise as his god, understood the riddle. He built the ship. The construction is described in detail. The ship is divided into different sections; within are stored all manner of silver and gold, seeds of every kind, his family and relatives, cattle, and even artisans. The last feature should be noted, which shows us that a civilized people is telling this story; according to another Babylonian recension, transmitted to us by a Greek hand,[5] the hero of the tale had actually buried writings in order to save them until the flood passed.

In what follows, the story of how the flood occurred is told with poetic, strongly mythical features. At the appointed time, Ut-Napištim himself enters the ship. A black cloud mounts up—the thundercloud of the god Hadad. Nebo and Marduk stride forward, and the Anunnaki raise their torches aloft. The waters rise and break loose on the people. The gods

---

delineation of the two sources, see Campbell and O'Brien, *The Sources of the Pentateuch*.

4. [Ed.] Ancient Šuruppak is now identified as Tell Fara in Iraq. See Martin, *Fara*; and Adams, *Heartland of Cities*.

5. [Ed.] Gunkel is evidently referring to the Babylonian author Berossus, who lived in the Hellenistic era.

Flood Tablet of the Gilgamesh Epic

themselves are terrified by the fearful flood; they flee on high to Anu's heaven and cower down there like dogs. Ištar, the divine mother of humans, cries loudly, and all the gods weep.

Finally the flood ceases. Ut-napištim opens the window; he looks out and laments the destruction of the world. The ship has settled firmly on a northern mountain. To learn whether the land is dry, he sends out birds three times: first a dove, which, however, finds no resting place and hence returns; then a swallow; and finally a raven. The raven sees the water receding and does not come back. That shows Ut-napištim that the earth is now dry.

He leaves the ship, and the first thing he does is offer a sacrifice. But the gods smell the savor and swarm like flies about the one who is sacrificing. Even Bel, the chief instigator of the flood, draws near. Ištar reproves him for doing so.

Bel grows angry as he sees the people who have survived the deluge. Ea half admits that he occasioned the rescue, and with vigorous irony recounts to Bel his folly in causing the flood. Finally Bel reconsiders and displays his favor to the rescued one by raising him among the gods.

The Babylonian story has been described here in detail in order that the reader might recognize its remarkable similarity to the biblical account, but at the same time its equally great divergence. In the first place, the points of contact: the similarity in the course of the events is immediately obvious—in spite of all divergences in detail, the substance of the story is the same on the whole. Particularly striking is the correspondence between the stories in the sending forth of the birds. How the heart of the first discoverer of the Babylonian narrative must have beaten when he came to this passage. The contact is also remarkable in that at the conclusion a sacrifice is offered and the gods smell the sacrifice. Other points occur as well, such as that in the second Hebrew source [P], as in the Greek-Babylonian tradition, Ararat (i.e., Armenia) is named as the landing-place of the ark. And the hero of the flood in both cases is the tenth of his line: Noah the tenth of the patriarchs, Ut-napištim the tenth of the kings. Accordingly, a relation must exist between the two *narratives*.

If we now consider the inconceivable antiquity of Babylonian civilization, and of this flood narrative as well, if we remember that floods are very natural precisely in Babylonia, which lies close to the sea and is a flat plain watered by great rivers, we cannot doubt that the Israelite story derived from the Babylonian. The Babylonian narrative of the great flood, as a piece of the great Babylonian civilization, has traveled throughout the world of the ancient Near East. We now have, in fact, the oldest representation of Noah's ark from a grave in ancient Etruria! A well-known attempt at evading this conclusion, due to overanxious temperaments and still appearing occasionally, should never have been made. That is, it is assumed that the Hebrew account is not dependent on the Babylonian but that both are versions of the same events. To everyone who knows legends, it is quite indubitable that the narratives, which correspond so in incidental details, must be related *as narratives.*

We say "to everyone who knows legends," for this conclusion is also unavoidable: the Hebrew tradition, if we derive it thus from the Babylonian, is not a historical narrative in the strict sense, but is poetic, popular—a legend. And, indeed, it is not only Assyriology that teaches us this, but the fact is evinced by entirely other characteristics, and should have been long obvious to everyone who lays claim to culture and good taste! The flood account is a legend, poetry, even as there are many kinds of poetry and many kinds of legends in the Old Testament as well. That is not the judgment of impiety and unbelief, but a judgment that is entirely compatible with piety and true devotion. For legends are the most precious treasure that an ancient people possesses, and they are particularly fitted to express the concepts of religion. What a melancholy spectacle it is if the angst-ridden piety of certain circles, in sad combination with a pitiful lack of culture, is afraid of the poetry of the Old Testament, the noblest poetry in the world! But from now on churches and schools should not leave the task of explaining to our people the legendary portions of the Old Testament to unbelievers. There is a pressing need that at least in the upper divisions of the higher schools, as soon as the possibility of historical intelligence has become manifest in the young people, it should be shown that poetic narratives are contained in the Old Testament through key examples; and the flood story might serve as a particularly apt example for this purpose.

We therefore agree absolutely with Delitzsch when he assumes the dependence of the biblical account of the flood on the Babylonian. Indeed, we regard it as no small merit that Delitzsch has been courageous enough to announce in the presence of that illustrious assembly this result of research, and, at the same time, to acknowledge without reserve his adherence to the modern criticism of the Pentateuch.[6] And the merit, which Delitzsch has so obtained for himself by popularizing research we shall not forget, even if we cannot agree with him in many other matters. For we certainly disagree with him even in the question as to *how* this dependence is to be regarded. Delitzsch seems here as in other cases to incline to the opinion that the biblical authors had the Babylonian legend lying before them in written form, and that it was translated and revised with full deliberation by them.[7] This opinion has too superficial a relation to the subject and for the student of the history of legends can hardly be considered. Much more probable is the assumption that the story came to Israel by oral tradition. And that this more natural assumption fits the situation here equally well is proved by the various deviations of the legendary *material* in the biblical and the Babylonian accounts. Thus, for example, the names "ark" [*tebha*, תבה] and "flood" [*mabbul*, מבול]—which, it is safe to

---

6. I:32 [46].
7. I:31 [45]; other instances below.

say, were not invented by the Hebrew writers—are different from the Babylonian.[8]

But much weightier than such an error is an omission that Delitzsch has disregarded. He has contented himself with establishing the *dependence* of the biblical matter on the Babylonian without including an investigation as to whether the biblical account as opposed to the original does not also have a true *independence*. And just on account of this omission, the impression might be created that the biblical account, since it is dependent on the Babylonian, is *worthless*! In fact Delitzsch himself has spoken of "the purer and more original form"[9] of the Babylonian traditions. This is an ominous one-sidedness inherent in Delitzsch's lectures, and on account of this he bears the chief blame in the reigning confusion! For where in all the world is it permitted merely to trace the origin of a subject without immediately adding, if it be at all possible, an investigation as to the manner in which the subject has been transformed? Our great German poets have repeatedly adopted old material for their greater creations: Goethe's *Faust*, for example, rests, as everyone knows, on an older German legend. But who thinks that Goethe's poetry is of lesser value if we have pointed out to us the book of folklore as the source of *Faust*? On the contrary, his power is seen for the first time when we observe what he has made of the clumsy and rough material.

8. Still, as Zimmern suggests to me, a connection is conceivable between the Babylonian *abûbu* and the Hebrew *mabbûl* [מבול]. [Ed.] Heinrich Zimmern (1862–1931) was Professor of Assyriology and Semitics at the University of Leipzig.

9. I:29 [42]; in the second edition Delitzsch has altered this expression, but again without adding a single word on the peculiar value of the Israelite tradition.

The same is true of the biblical and Babylonian stories of the flood. The difference between the two is almost immeasurable; different worlds are expressed in them. In the Babylonian story, a wild, grotesque polytheism: the gods out-scheme and combat one another; they quake before the flood, cower like dogs in the heavens, and come like flies to the sacrifice. But the biblical story speaks of the one God, whose just retribution sends the flood, and who graciously protects the pious man after he has tested him. The biblical narrative, therefore, also lacks a trait contained in the Babylonian, and which is perhaps pleasing to modern sentimental sensibilities, namely, the sympathy of the hero for the drowned men. But what an exaggeration when Delitzsch asserts that the Babylonian legend, on account of this one feature, "appeals to us with far greater force than the biblical narrative!"[10] And our sympathy with this feature, moreover, will be markedly diminished when we add that it in no way occurred to the hero of the flood to warn his fellow citizens, but rather—barbarously enough— instead of warning them, he announced to them an abundant blessing—and that on the advice of his god! But the narrative of the Bible, which bases the deluge on the sins of humanity, is entirely too *earnest* to know pity for *justly* punished sinners. Accordingly, the Israelite tradition had by no means simply adopted the Babylonian. On the contrary, it utterly transformed the story; a true marvel of the world's history, it has changed dross into gold. Should we not then as Christians rejoice, that in these early Babylonian recensions we have found a line to measure how much the God in whom we believe was nearer to ancient Israel than to the Babylonians? Truly, the

10. II:33 [200].

one who has a sense for religion and the history of religion cannot overlook this powerful difference between the two narratives.

Creation Narratives

The situation is similar regarding the creation narratives, except that here the proof for the dependence of the Israelite tradition in Genesis 1 upon the Babylonian is much harder to produce. The creation narrative of the Babylonians recounts how the world was originally a great expanse of water, which the Babylonians, in their mythological style, represent as a powerful female primeval being, Tiamat. All the gods originated from the union of Tiamat with the primeval father, Apsû. Now the myth tells how a struggle arose between the younger and the older gods, until finally Marduk, the city-god of Babylon, overcame Tiamat, cut her into two parts, and made heaven and earth from them. So the earth was formed from the primeval waters.[11]

Whoever compares this primal Babylonian myth with Genesis 1 will at first grasp hardly anything but the infinite gulf between the two.[12] On the one hand, the heathen deities are inflamed in a wild struggle against one another; on the other is the one who speaks, and it comes to pass. Nonetheless, there are certain traces that make it probable to us that the Babylonian account lies behind the biblical, even if both must have been separated by a very long period of time.

11. [Ed.] See Foster, *Before the Muses*; and Dalley, *Myths from Mesopotamia*, 228–77.

12. [Ed.] For Gunkel's fuller analysis of Gen 1:1—2:4a, see his commentary, *Genesis*, 103–33.

Marduk attacking Tiamat

The account in Hebrew has several remnants that show us that it must have been mythical at one time; here also the world was originally water, and the expression *tehom* (תהום), which is used here, is ultimately the same as the Babylonian *Tiamat*. And in the Hebrew account, also, the world is created so that the original primeval waters are divided into two parts, heaven and earth. Accordingly, in spite of all discrepancies between the religious ideas, related material! Now here, too, the dependence of the Hebrew on the Babylonian is probable; for the manner in which the world arises corresponds entirely to the Babylonian climate, in which in the winter water holds sway everywhere until the god of the spring sun appears, who parts the water and creates heaven and earth. But that the story of the struggle of the light-god against the waters of the primeval age and against the wild monsters was known in Canaan as well, is shown by certain references by prophets, poets, and apocalyptists, where this struggle has been transferred to Yahweh.[13] Such references are valuable in this connection because they represent the links between the grotesque Babylonian primal myth and the late Hebrew account of Genesis 1. Accordingly, we can also assume a dependence of Genesis 1 on the Babylonian account, with regard to the content; but the original portions far outweigh those that were taken over. Therefore, this assumption also serves only to show the unique height of Israel's religion.

But again this consideration teaches us that the story of creation, no less than that of the deluge, is a *poem.* No one who cares about our church should strive against this acknowledgment. It would not be too much to hope for, and it would be the beginning of a highly necessary reformation, if in the book of biblical history the first section would be headed "The Poem of Creation." May students consider this suggestion. There is still time. Perhaps the hour is coming when it will be said *too late!*

The tradition of the primeval patriarchs of humanity prior to the flood is, as may be assumed with great probability, of Babylonian origin: the Hebrew names can in part be regarded as direct translations of the names of Babylonian kings. This explanation is significant, because in this way a light falls on the great ages ascribed to the patriarchs, which have given rise to such discussions. The Babylonian tradition

13. The principal passages are Pss 104:5ff.; 46:3–4; Isa 17:12–14; 51:9–10; Pss 89:10ff.; Job 26:12; 9:13; Ps 74:12ff.; Isa 27:1; Daniel 7; Revelation 12, 13, 17. One will find a more complete discussion of these passages in my work *Creation and Chaos*, 21–77 [*Schöpfung und Chaos*, 29–114]. [Ed.] Gunkel's argument is basically confirmed now in the Ugaritic myths of Baal's defeat of Judge River/Prince Sea (*špṭ nhr /śr ymm*).

contains in this place even greater numbers, and these are explained by an astronomical chronology of the world.

Of the primal myths of the Bible, Delitzsch has designated paradise as Babylonian as well, but only on the ground of an Old Babylonian picture [on a cylinder-seal], whose meaning is entirely uncertain. Delitzsch's remark on the distinction of sources in the paradise story is surprising;[14] one can find in the biblical narrative of Genesis 2:4b—3:24 another and older form that recognized only one tree in the middle of the garden—*the Tree of Life*. But this supposition that an older recension of the story knew of only a single tree has been expressed already and long ago (by Karl Budde), and is known almost universally. But critics have usually assumed that this single tree was the *Tree of Knowledge*. Are Delitzsch's words here simply rhetorical? Or does he really think that he has succeeded in saying something substantive? If the latter is the case, he should have expounded and sustained his opinion more fully; the arguments that he uses have been employed for other purposes up to the present.[15]

Miscellaneous Traditions

Following Eberhard Schrader, Delitzsch further compares the legend of the *madness of Nebuchadnezzar*, who on account of his pride was driven from men and lived with the beasts of the field [Dan 4:28–33], with a Greco-Babylonian tradition, according to which the king, at the height of his power,

14. I:67 [114].

15. [Ed.] For Gunkel's detailed treatment of Gen 2:4b—3:24, see his commentary, *Genesis*, 4–40. Karl Budde (1850–1935) was Professor of Old Testament at the universities of Bonn, Strasbourg, and Marburg.

Gilgamesh

predicted a foreign conqueror and wished that he [the con-
queror] might be hunted through the desert, where the wild
beasts and birds roam. Both traditions have a certain similarity; but this is certainly much too weak to safely assert a
dependence of the biblical upon the Babylonian. Much closer
is the connection of the Jewish legend with the Babylonian
Eabani,[16] who lived among the beasts like a beast; his hair
covered his whole body, and spread out like wheat stalks, and
he ate grass with the gazelles. And here, too, Delitzsch follows
the superficial conception that the *author* revised the foreign
legend;[17] the question could be, at the most, a transformation

16. [Ed.] This is an early, spurious transliteration of "Enkidu," the
name of Gilgamesh's friend and companion.

17. II:15 [168].

in *oral* tradition—I believe that all folklorists will agree with me in that. But Delitzsch actually wants the Babylonian origin and "the purer and more original form of this story" to be imparted to children as soon as they hear of the corresponding biblical story! But the startling expression that we have been "burdened by tradition" through the representation of the madness of the "brutified" Nebuchadnezzar ought to have been avoided in any case. Did Delitzsch ever regard this narrative as anything *but* a legend?

The same is true regarding everything he marshals in such a flowery way on the origin of belief in a *life after death*—dubious in the extreme. Rather the ancient Babylonians and Hebrews concurred in the belief that after death the soul enters the dark underworld from which there is no rescue for ordinary people.[18] The belief in resurrection does not belong in general to the Old Testament, but arose first in the postcanonical era, and, in any case, not under the influence of the ancient Babylonian religion.

It is correct that the *belief in angels* recalls Babylonian views, particularly in the belief as it appears in postexilic Judaism; we can prove that for the seven archangels and surmise it for the seraphim and cherubim.[19] But whether the belief in angels *in general* originated from Babylonia is another question, which may well be propounded provisionally, but which can scarcely be answered.

The derivation of the Hebrew sabbath from the Babylonian has stirred up much dust. Here also we must warn the laity against unnecessary excitement, for what is the sabbath

18. [Ed.] The ancient Israelites called this Sheol (שׁאול). See Lewis, "Dead, Abode of the."

19. [Ed.] See Mettinger, "Cherubim"; Mettinger, "Seraphim."

to us? The high and pure religion of Christianity, as it has been renewed in Luther's Reformation, knows no holy days! Jesus boldly transgressed the sabbath law, and the apostle says: "Therefore do not let anyone condemn you in matters of food and drink, or of observing festivals, new moons, or sabbaths" (Col 2:16). The Christian observance of Sunday is not a carryover of the sabbath but something new and different.

According to the history of religion, however, the case is this. The observance of such a holy day in the great historical religion is a remnant of an older era, when people believed in gods who, *according to their nature*, belonged to certain days. This quite clear for the new moon festival, which naturally originally correlated to the veneration of the moon. We have not learned the history of the origin of the sabbath from the Babylonian discoveries; for such cultic institutions are generally much too old for so late a people as Israel to provide a historic tradition of their origin. So it is not remarkable if even the most ancient Israel knew as little of the origin of the sabbath as of circumcision, abstaining from blood, and many other ceremonies.[20] But if there are, nevertheless, explanations in Israel of such customs—as for the sabbath the well-known explanation that the sabbath is holy because God hallowed it by resting after the creation—those explanations are supplied *after the fact*. And while they may be as spiritual and deep as can be, they do not come into consideration for the explanation of the ceremonies themselves.

20. Delitzsch (I:128 [40]), who does not seem to occupy himself with investigations in the history of religion, finds it "significant" that Israelite tradition itself no longer affords any certain information respecting the origin of the Sabbath; the student of that field finds it simply *self-evident*. For a more recent summary of the data see Hasel, "Sabbath."

Accordingly, if we find among the Babylonians any parallel for the sabbath, we shall simply rejoice over the enrichment of our knowledge. And we may assume such parallels, even with a certain provisional reserve,[21] and suppose that the Hebrew sabbath originated from Babylonia, the classic land for the honor of the planets and their characteristic days. But it is certainly again a gross overstatement when Delitzsch says that we owe the blessings contained in the sabbath (or Sunday) rest to that ancient civilization.[22] For such days, on the other hand, take on an entirely different character when they pass over into a different religion! The ancient Babylonians observed the sabbath as a day of fasting, on which angry deities had to be propitiated, as a malevolent day when certain transactions should be avoided. The ancient Hebrew sabbath contains nothing of such ideas but was held as a joyous holiday. And how can one actually say of Sunday that its wealth of blessings originally derived from Babylon?

We pass over all these minor matters, of which many more might still be named,[23] and come to the primary question, whether and to what extent the Babylonians were *monotheists*. Here one must, in the first place, state that there have been different forms of monotheism among various peoples

21. Cf. Zimmern, *Keilinschriften und das Alte Testament*, 592ff.

22. I:29 [41].

23. The material, which Delitzsch arrays in the comparison of the two religions, is of very different natures; partly it contains portions in which Israel is dependent on Babylon; partly, cases where a certain similarity is observed without dependence being necessary on that account; often the similarities are so general that they are found everywhere in antiquity, as, for example, that the deity reveals Itself in a dream or through an intermediary. Such cases would not have been mentioned at all in this connection by an investigator trained in the history of religion.

and at various times. But in spite of that, the people of Israel are and remain the classic people of monotheism. This monotheism that we know, or more exactly, which was our precursor, originates from Judaism; and in Israel this monotheism originated entirely independently. We know the history of its origin in Israel very well. *The religion of Babylon is, on the other hand, unquestionably polytheistic*; and in fact it has a thoroughly crass, grotesque pantheon. If something should be found in Babylon that is reminiscent of monotheism, that is the exception. *The great historic effect that results from it is, at this point, not due to Babylon, but to Israel.*

Delitzsch has referred to several details; to begin with, to certain names compounded with, *ʾel* = God, such as "God with me," "I call upon God," "God is great," etc., which were used especially among northern Semitic immigrants at the time of Hammurabi. Delitzsch assumes that these northern Semites were related to the Hebrews, and like these were monotheists from the most ancient period. His opinion is consequently in no way that *Israelite* monotheism *originated* in Babylonia. And in the meantime all these combinations have a hollow ring, something Delitzsch could have learned from anyone who knows the history of religion. The polytheistic Greeks, for example, had names like *Theophilos* = "beloved of God," *Theopompos* = "sent by God," *Theodosios* = "gift of God," *Theoxenos* = "guest-friend of God," etc. The similarly polytheistic Phoenicians, Aramaeans, and Arabs have numerous names that are compounded with *ʾel* = God: such as *ʿAimel* = "eye of God," *Channel* = "grace of God," *ʿAliel* = "God is exalted," etc.[24] It may also be remarked in passing that everything that Delitzsch observes regarding the Babylonian

24. Cf. Chamberlain, *Dilettantismus*, 44ff.; Meyer, "El."

name *Yahu-ilu* = "Yahweh is God,"[25] is dubious in the extreme. The whole reading or meaning is, in the judgment of many of Delitzsch's Assyriological colleagues, very questionable.[26] But in the distinguished venue in which Delitzsch spoke—this we ought not to refrain from saying—he should have taken the greatest care to utter only assured facts.

There is still a text from the Neo-Babylonian period in which various gods are equated with Marduk; and along with Delitzsch, this is to be regarded as nearly monotheistic.[27] From this text it is shown that Babylonian priestly wisdom, at a certain point of history, recognized that the different deities are, in the end, manifestations of the same divine essence—a view that Greek popular philosophy also held at the time of Jesus. We are glad for such a spiritual height, which towers aloft through all the confused folly of polytheism up to the One. Certainly such an understanding of the sages in Babylonia affected actual religion as little in Babylonia as in Greece, where religion remained polytheistic. So this monotheistic *speculation* is to be compared with the monotheistic *religion* of Israel only distantly.

The reader will have noticed that up to this point we have spoken only of pure details. There is a good reason for

25. I:46ff. [71].

26. Zimmern, *Keilinschriften und das Alte Testament*, 468. On the etymology of Yahweh and El, cf. above, p. 18 and n. 15. Moreover, in itself there certainly can be nothing to argue against the occurrence of the name Yahweh in pre-Israelite times, for Moses certainly did not invent the name. We might rather assume, even without evidence, that the name had some sort of a previous history. Why shouldn't it occur somewhere in the Babylonian pantheon as well? But the question is not about the sound "Yahweh," but as to what sort of a divine figure people conceived relative to this name.

27. Zimmern, *Keilinschriften und das Alte Testament*, 609.

this. Currently, Babylonian religion is known to us only frag-
mentarily, while the Israelite certainly lies before us clearly
in its essential features and its historical epochs. So what we
can give at the present, if we want to discuss the influence of
Babylonia on the religion of Israel, is then, at the most, that we
define (naturally with all due reserve) those *domains* in which
a transfer of more or less religious matter from Babylon to
Israel can have taken place. Those are

- legends and myths above all;

- institutions of civilization, which are, perhaps to
  great extent, Babylonian in origin;

- legal statutes, which indeed in antiquity were always
  connected in some way with religion;

- cosmology, the conceptions of the nature and divisions of the world;

- popular beliefs regarding heavenly, terrestrial, and
  underworld beings of all sorts—angels and demons;

- computations of the duration and epochs of the
  world, prophetic and apocalyptic imagery;

- the most valuable pieces are perhaps religious songs,
  which have wandered through the lands in connection with cultic regulations; we have Babylonian
  psalms, which, even if vastly inferior religiously to the
  Hebrew, are nonetheless related to them in form.[28]

---

28. [Ed.] See Gunkel's work on the Psalms, which was completed
posthumously thirty years following the present work: *Introduction
to the Psalms*. Throughout this work he makes comparisons with
Babylonian and Egyptian poetry and songs.

But most of this material, at least in Israel, is connected only loosely with actual religion; or else, as we have seen in the narratives of the flood and creation, and as can be easily shown in the religious songs, has been made Israelite in the strongest fashion. If we view the essential and determinative facts, we must acknowledge that *Israel's religion in the classical period is independent over against Babylon.*

Likewise one cannot as yet draw a *parallel between the two religions.* Delitzsch has attempted it, but has remained stuck in details. And in the process—we appeal in this matter to the judgment of all experts—he has conducted himself in an entirely partisan manner. He exalts the Babylonian and debases Israel as far as possible. So it is a great injustice when Delitzsch asserts that "the same naïve representations of the deity" are found in Israel and Babylon.[29] Just as the Babylonian gods eat and drink and even rest, so Yahweh goes forth in the cool of the evening to walk in paradise and takes pleasure in the sweet scent of Noah's sacrifice. But now there can be no doubt to the unprejudiced judge that the idea the Babylonian had of God was *by far* more naïve than the Israelite. One need think only of the manner in which the gods appear in the story of the flood, where they cower like dogs in heaven. The Old Testament also occasionally includes marked anthropomorphisms; but these are in no way as crass as is customary in Babylon. Historical Israel never described Yahweh eating and drinking. Overt anthropomorphisms are *archaisms* in the Old Testament, which have remained in the primeval legends of the flood and of paradise, but which have been superseded by the more advanced religion.

29. II:175.

Delitzsch's method may be excusable since he was angered by the injudicious zeal of certain theological opponents. But we wish not to be partisan, but as objective and as just as possible. We certainly have no intention of glossing over Israel's obvious weaknesses, which occasionally come to expression in the Old Testament. And neither do we have any need of finding everything noble and beautiful in Israel. Jewish monotheism, for example, this we frankly admit, is frequently sullied by a hate, and often a blood-red hatred for the heathen, a fact that we may understand historically from the miserable condition of the continually oppressed Jews, but one which we in no case wish to adopt into our religion. Someone may defend the prayer "pour out your wrath upon the heathen," but we don't. On the other hand, we certainly do not wish to combat what the Babylonians have achieved, least of all in religion. The hymns of the Babylonians to their great gods, which often rise to a high pitch, and their penitential psalms, in which a strong feeling of sin often resounds, meet a receptive ear in us. We rejoice over the ancient, admirable civilization of this people, from whom Israel could have learned much.

But if the Babylonian and biblical religions are to be compared, what nonpartisan observer can doubt with which side he is to align himself?

- Crass *polytheism* compared, in the classical era, to *monotheism*;
- the Babylonian religion replete with witchcraft, which lies deep under the feet of the great prophets of Israel;

- the cult of *images* compared to strict iconoclasm in the Jewish cult;[30]

- the association of the gods with nature compared to religious thought that rises, in the classical period, to the belief in one God, who stands above the world;

- religious prostitution, which once overran Israel as well, but that is abhorred through the holy fury of the prophets!

The fairest possession of Israel, however, is the theme of her prophets, that God desires no offering or ceremonies, but piety of the heart and righteousness of deeds. This innermost connection of religion with morality is the primary reason Israel's religion rises above all other religions of the ancient Near East! This is Israel's legacy to humanity, and it remains so, even if Judaism has become again untrue to this mighty idea.

And where does the Babylonian world have characters like the great religious figures of the prophets: the indignant Amos, the majestic Isaiah, the deep and tender Jeremiah, to say absolutely nothing of Moses and Elijah? The prophets of Israel during the exile felt themselves superior to the religion of Babylon, which they had before their eyes, despite

30. In order to make the idolatry of the Babylonians understandable, Delitzsch refers to the fact that even the prophets of Israel represented Yahweh anthropomorphically (II:30ff. [195]). Quite right; the idea of the "immateriality" of God is striven for but not yet attained. But what a great advance it is, nevertheless, that the prophetic religion repels every image with lofty scorn! And in that regard we are children of the prophets and not of the Babylonians. But how can Delitzsch, in this connection, actually point to the images of God the Father in Christian art? For every child among us knows what the Babylonians did *not* know: that such pictures are not really true pictures of the Deity, but are mere works of imagination.

the pomp and splendor with which it was clothed, despite the fact that these gods were the gods of the world empire, despite the fact that Judah was thrown in the dust. They certainly have not judged it *justly*, even as is likely to happen in the struggle of religions; but fundamentally they were right. Bel has fallen and Nebo has been overthrown; but through the millennia resounds the joyous shout of Israel's singer: "Who, O Yahweh, is like you among the gods?"[31] The gods of the Babylonians passed away when their time came. The hearts of the heathen turned to the God of little Judah when the time was fulfilled. This enormous historical event, under whose influence the whole of subsequent world history stands, must have had a most mighty cause. And what is this cause? What else can it be other than the decisive superiority of this religion over the others?

31. [Ed.] Exod 15:11; variations on this formula appear throughout the Old Testament; cf. Deut 33:26; 2 Sam 7:22; Ps 86:8; and Isa 46:9.

6

Revelation in Israel

And now at the conclusion, the question: *May we continue to speak of the revelation of God in Israel?* Delitzsch has denied it. In this regard it is surely seen most clearly that he lacks actual theological training. His position, therefore, is unclear and inadequate. We will attempt to clarify his viewpoint in the hope of dealing appropriately with at least the primary issue. The conception of revelation that he postulates is the *supernatural*, old ecclesiastical theory, which one is still accustomed to associate popularly with this word. According to this, "revelation" stands in conceptual contrast to everything human. The proposition that Old Testament religion is "revelation" consequently excludes in this sense all human cooperation and historical development.

Delitzsch struggles to refute this proposition that Old Testament religion rests upon revelation in this sense, and he does it by pointing to all kinds of contradictions and difficulties in the Old Testament. For instance, he shows that the God who despises all external sacrifice, according to testimony of the prophets, could not possibly have prescribed the ceremonial law of the later Jewish legislation in the so-called Priestly Code. Or he points to the numerous heathen parallels to Old Testament law: sabbath, new moons, the bread of presence, and circumcision are the property not only of Israel, but of other people as well. Or he shows that there are also purely secular works in the Old Testament, such as the Song of Songs, a collection of Hebrew love songs, which can scarcely have anything at all to do with religion.

We may adopt this line of argument of Delitzsch most appropriately, even if we must take exception in some particulars. We hail Delitzsch as a colleague in the battle against the delusion of assuming that the Old Testament is verbally inspired, as though its religion had in some way fallen from heaven, and had grown without human cooperation and without history. Only, most assuredly, we hail him without burdening ourselves in any way with this, largely superficial and even uncivil, line of argument. For this colleague comes somewhat late. The theologian who knows the history of his discipline knows that such polemics against supernaturalism have existed for two centuries, and often have been uttered with much greater material than the modest collection that Delitzsch has hastily raked together. And these century-old polemics bore their fruit years ago. The opponents whom Delitzsch combats no longer exist—at least not in academic circles. And the doors he breaks down with such exquisite zeal have stood open for years. Theology has on all sides dropped that orthodox belief in inspiration, and dropped it long ago. Likewise, the belief that ancient Israelite religion arose, not historically, but *purely super*historically, *super*naturally, is defended by hardly a single Protestant German theologian. That is not unknown even to Delitzsch. There are remnants of the old view yet at work, sometimes in circles that are not very acquainted with academic theology. And frequently, even among theologians, the principal difference between the old supernatural theory and the modern based on the history of religion is not recognized with full clarity. People often satisfy themselves with half-compromises. So we may leave Delitzsch unmolested in this opinion; only let him choose his terms more gently, as is befitting when one deals with such holy things, and let him not indulge in the opinion that he has "opened up" an important theological question.[1]

But now Delitzsch thinks he has overthrown *revelation entirely* by proving "revelation" in this sense to be impossible. "Revelation" to him is nothing but the supernatural; he certainly knows that another concept of revelation has existed among theologians for a long time; but he can regard this as only a "dilution" of the old ecclesiastical belief.[2]

How does it stand regarding this modern conceptuality of revelation? We say in advance that in discussing such a subject we shall leave the realm of historical research and speak on the question of how the historical is to be judged from the standpoint of *religion*, of *faith*. Now contemporary academic theology believes it possesses a deeper understanding of revelation, according to which the divine and the human do not exist together in mere *external* relations, but are bound together *internally*. The history of revelation proceeds, therefore, among people, according to the same psychological laws as govern other human events. But in the depth of this

1. II:41 [213].
2. II:44 [219].

event the eye of *faith* sees God, who speaks to the soul and who reveals himself to the one who seeks him with a whole heart. We recognize God's revelation in the great persons of religion, who receive the holy secret in their innermost parts and announce it with tongues of flame. We see God's revelation in the great changes and wonderful providences of history. The faith of children, both ancient and contemporary, thinks that God wrote the tables of the law with his own hand and passed them to Moses; the faith of the adult and mature person knows that God writes his commandments with his finger on the hearts of his servants.[3]

Do we now have the right to see such a revelation in Israel's religion? Certainly! For what sort of a religion is it? *A true miracle of God's among the religions of the ancient Near East!* What streams flow here of overwhelming enthusiasm for the majestic God, of deep reverence before his holy sway, and of intrepid trust in his faithfulness! The one who looks upon this religion with believing eyes will confess with us: God has disclosed himself to this people! Here God was more closely and clearly known than anywhere else in the ancient Near East, until the time of Jesus Christ our Lord! This is the religion on which we are dependent, from which we continuously learn, on whose foundation our whole civilization is built. We are Israelites in religion, even as we are Greeks in art and Romans in law. Then if the Israelites are far beneath the Babylonians in many matters of civilization, nonetheless they are far above them in religion. *Israel is and remains the people of revelation.* Now is that really a "dilution" of the concept of

3. [Ed.] For contemporary discussions, see, e.g., Dulles, *Models of Revelation*; and Gunton, *A Brief Theology of Revelation*.

revelation, as Delitzsch thinks? No, we believe that that is a *spiritualization and deepening of it*!

But psychologically, Delitzsch may be understood as follows: In the circles from which he comes and in which he was formerly educated in theology, he acquired only a rather crass—or to say it in plain but vigorous language—a rather *mythological* concept of revelation. And now that he recognizes the untenability of such opinions, he turns against this conceptuality with zeal and anger without having attained a satisfactory attitude towards both research and religion. Such a result is common in such cases. So during his year away,[4] he allowed himself to be driven by these theological opponents into a much more dogmatic position than the one he originally assumed. For in his first lecture he uttered the watchword that we have yet to free the religion of the prophets, psalmists, and Jesus from "purely human conceptions" that still cling to this religion.[5] At that time he seems to have still believed that the religion of the prophets, as such, was not "purely human." Even now he distinguishes in the book of Jonah the "human form" from the proper content; the content, accordingly, if we understand Delitzsch rightly, is *not* "human."[6]

It is conceivable that Delitzsch wishes to cause harm to our faith in God and true religiosity by his denial of revelation.[7] But is our faith in God imaginable without the belief that this God reveals himself to humanity within history? Or does Delitzsch acknowledge in Jesus an absolutely supernatu-

4. [Ed.] Gunkel is evidently referring to the year Delitzsch spent in the Middle East.

5. I:44 [67].

6. II:16 [170].

7. II:39 [211].

ral revelation? We may perhaps assume so from the manner
in which he speaks of Jesus. In any case, it will be a great
inconsistency if he admits an exception into his worldview—
for that, and not details, is the real issue. In one place Delitzsch
holds that the modern theological conception—that all divine revelation is through human intermediaries and hence
is a gradual development—is his own as well.[8] So he is finally
in complete agreement with us? But even on the same page
he retracts this view.[9] And in another place he speaks of the
revelation of God that we, each one of us, carry in our own
consciences,[10] which is, accordingly, even if very rational-
istically expressed, a nonsupernatural revelation, which he
combats elsewhere. A very labyrinth of contradictions! On
what theological height Delitzsch stands is evinced by such
utterances of his as: "*Is there then a belief besides the Biblical
belief?*"[11]—one can hardly believe one's eyes when reading
it. Or even: "Humankind has certainly not *deserved* a personal divine revelation on account of his trifling with the Ten
Commandments"[12]—what an impossible idea! For what have
we ever "deserved" from God?

If we understand Delitzsch correctly, he is a rationalist
of the old school, who has freed himself from an earlier supernaturalism and in exasperation fights this as his proper
foe—although some bits of the shell of supernaturalism cling
to him even now—but who has not yet arrived at the understanding that *history* is the proper domain of revelation.

8. II:44 [219].
9. II:44 [219].
10. II:20 [178].
11. I:59 [?].
12. II:20 [178].

We cannot refrain from asserting that such an unhistorical rationalism is nearly the most arid conception of religion that has ever existed, and that previously we had indulged in the illusion that such a theological position was demolished and would not reappear.

What will the future of the whole "Babel and Bible" movement be? One may predict with great certainty: the sensation will be followed, in the not too distant future, by disillusionment; a new newsworthy event will displace "Babel and Bible." Even Delitzsch's lectures, which have neither added new material nor been able to say anything especially novel in theology, will soon be forgotten by the public. And future histories of research will hardly mention them. But what survives as a consequence of the whole disturbance is, we may hope, an enduring interest of the educated in Babylonian and biblical research. For this we must thank Delitzsch in spite of all the contradictions we have been compelled to provide. But from now on let interested individuals make use of solid and expertly unassailable publications. But at the same time there remains, we fear, a mistrust in wide circles against the Church, which has, alas, so long ignored theological research and its assured results. May the Protestant Church draw a lesson from contemporary events and become conscious of its task, to present the faith to the community in such a form that no historical criticism may assail it.

Bibliography

Gunkel's References

Chamberlain, Houston Stewart. *Dilettantismus, Rasse, Monotheismus, Rom.* 4th ed. Munich: Bruckmann, 1903.

Delitzsch, Friedrich. *Babel and Bible: Two Lectures Delivered before the Members of the Deutsche Orientgesellschaft in the Presence of the German Emperor.* Edited with an Introduction by C. H. W. John. 1902. Reprinted, ANECS. Eugene, OR: Wipf & Stock, 2007.

———. *Babel and Bible: Three Lectures on the Significance of Assyriological Research for Religion, Embodying the Most Important Criticisms and the Author's Replies.* Translated by Thomas J. McCormack, W. H. Carruth, and Lydia G. Robinson. Chicago: Open Court, 1906.

———. *Babel und Bibel.* Leipzig: Hinrichs, 1902.

———. *Zweiter Vortrag zum Babel und Bibel.* Stuttgart: Verlags-Anstalt, 1903.

Gunkel, Hermann. "Babylonische und biblische Urgeschichte." *Christliche Welt* 6 (1903) 121–34.

———. *Creation and Chaos in the Primeval Era and the Eschaton: Religio-Historical Study of Genesis 1 and Revelation 12.* Translated by K. William Whitney Jr. Biblical Resources Series. Grand Rapids: Eerdmans, 2006.

———. *Genesis.* Handkommentar zum Alten Testament. 3rd ed. Göttingen: Vandenhoeck & Ruprecht, 1910.

———. *Genesis.* Translated by Mark E. Biddle. Mercer Library of Biblical Studies. Macon, GA: Mercer University Press, 1977.

———. *Schöpfung und Chaos in Urzeit und Endzeit: Eine religions-geschichtliche Untersuchung über Gen. 1 und Ap. Joh. 12.* Göttingen: Vandenhoeck & Ruprecht, 1895.

Meyer, Eduard. "El." In *Ausführliches Lexikon der römischen und griechischen Mythologie*, edited by W. H. Roscher. Vol. 1/1. Leipzig: Teubner, 1886.

Zimmern, Heinrich. "Part 2: Religion und Sprache." In Eberhard Schrader, *Keilinschriften und das Alte Testament*. 3rd ed. Berlin: Reuther & Reichard, 1903.

Editor's References

Adams, Robert McC. *Heartland of Cities: Surveys of Ancient Settlement and Land Use on the Central Floodplain of the Euphrates*. Chicago: University of Chicago Press, 1981.

Alster, Bendt. "Tiamat." In *DDD*, 867–69.

Arnold, Bill T., and David B. Weisberg. "A Centennial Review of Friedrich Delitzsch's 'Babel und Bibel' Lectures." *Journal of Biblical Literature* 121 (2002) 441–57.

Brooke, George J. et al., editors. *Ugarit and the Bible: Proceedings of the International Symposium on Ugarit and the Bible, Manchester, September 1992*. Ugaritisch-Biblische Literatur 11. Münster: Ugarit-Verlag, 1994.

Burkert, Walter. *The Orientalizing Revolution: Near Eastern Influence on Greek Culture in the Early Archaic Age*. Translated by Walter Burkert and Margaret E. Pinder. Revealing Antiquity 5. Cambridge: Harvard University Press, 1992.

Burstein, Stanley Mayer, editor and translator. *The Babyloniaca of Berossus*. Sources from the Ancient Near East 1/5. Malibu, CA: Undena, 1978.

Campbell, Antony F., and Mark A. O'Brien. *The Sources of the Pentateuch: Texts, Introductions, Annotations*. Minneapolis: Fortress, 1993.

Carus, Paul. "Gunkel vs. Delitzsch." *The Open Court* 18 (1904) 226–41.

Chavalas, Mark W., and K. Lawson Younger Jr., editors. *Mesopotamia and the Bible: Comparative Explorations*. Grand Rapids: Baker Academic, 2002.

Cross, Frank Moore. *Canaanite Myth and Hebrew Epic: Essays in the History of the Religion of Israel*. Cambridge: Harvard University Press, 1973.

––––––. "אל *El*." In *TDOT* 1 (1974) 259–79.

Dalley, Stephanie. *Myths from Mesopotamia: Creation, the Flood, Gilgamesh, and Others*. The World's Classics. Oxford: Oxford University Press, 1989.

Delitzsch, Friedrich. *Die Grosse Täuschung*. Stuttgart: Deutsche Verlags-Anstalt, 1921.

Dulles, Avery. *Models of Revelation*. With a new Preface. Maryknoll, NY: Orbis, 1992.

Ericksen, Robert P., and Susannah Heschel, editors. *Betrayal: German Churches and the Holocaust*. Minneapolis: Fortress, 1999.

Evans, Carl D. et al., editors. *Essays on the Comparative Method*. Scripture in Context 1. Pittsburgh Theological Monograph Series 34. Pittsburgh: Pickwick, 1980.

Fisher, Loren R., editor. *Ras Shamra Parallels: The Texts from Ugarit and the Hebrew Bible*. Vols. 1–2. AnOr 49, 50. Rome: Pontifical Biblical Institute Press, 1972, 1975.

Foster, Benjamin R. *Before the Muses: An Anthology of Akkadian Literature*. 3rd ed. Baltimore: CDL, 2005.

———. "Epic of Creation." In *COS*, 1:390–402.

Freedman, David Noel, and Michael Patrick O'Conner. "יהוה *YHWH*." In *TDOT* 5 (1986) 500–520.

George, Andrew. *The Epic of Gilgamesh*. New York: Penguin, 2003.

Greenfield, Jonas C. "Aspects of Aramean Religion." In *AIR*, 67–78.

Gunkel, Hermann. *The Folktale in the Old Testament*. Translated by Michael D. Rutter. Introduction by John W. Rogerson. Historic Texts and Interpreters in Biblical Scholarship. Sheffield: Almond, 1987.

———. "The Hagar Traditions." In *Water for a Thirsty Land: Israelite Literature and Religion*, edited by K. C. Hanson, 68–84. Fortress Classics in Biblical Studies. Minneapolis: Fortress, 2001.

———. *Creation and Chaos in the Primeval Era and the Eschaton: Religio-Historical Study of Genesis 1 and Revelation 12*. Translated by K. William Whitney Jr. Biblical Resources Series. Grand Rapids: Eerdmans, 2006.

———. *Genesis*. Translated by Mark E. Biddle. Mercer Library of Biblical Studies. Macon, GA: Mercer University Press, 1977.

———. *Introduction to the Psalms: The Genres of the Religious Lyric of Israel*. Completed by Joachim Begrich. Translated by James D. Nogalski. Mercer Library of Biblical Studies. Macon, GA: Mercer University Press, 1998.

———. *Water for a Thirsty Land: Israelite Literature and Religion*. Edited by K. C. Hanson. Fortress Classics in Biblical Studies. Minneapolis: Fortress, 2001.

Gunton, Colin. *A Brief Theology of Revelation: The 1993 Warfield Lectures*. New York: Continuum, 2005.

Hallo, William W. "Compare and Contrast: The Contextual Approach to Biblical Literature." In *The Bible in Light of Cuneiform Literature*, edited by William W. Hallo et al., 1–30. Studies in Context 3. Ancient Near Eastern Texts and Studies 8. Lewiston, NY: Mellen, 1990.

————. "Introduction: Ancient Near Eastern Texts and Their Relevance for Biblical Exegesis." In *COS*, 1:xxiii–xxviii.

Hallo, William W. et al., editors. *More Essays on the Comparative Method.* Scripture in Context 2. Winona Lake, IN: Eisenbrauns, 1983.

Hanson, K. C. "Parallels and Connections between the Hellenic, Semitic, and Anatolian Cultures." Online: www.kchanson.com/CLASSIFIEDBIB/anegreek.html.

Harper, Robert Francis. *The Code of Hammurabi: King of Babylon, about 2250 B.C.* 1904. Reprinted, ATT. Eugene, OR: Wipf & Stock, 2007.

Hasel, Gerhard F. "Sabbath." In *ABD* 5:848–56.

Herrmann, Wolfgang. "Baal." In *DDD*, 132–39.

————. "El." In *DDD*, 274–80.

Heschel, Susannah. *Abraham Geiger and the Jewish Jesus.* Chicago Studies in the History of Judaism. Chicago: University of Chicago Press, 1998.

Hess, Richard S., and David Toshio Tsumura, editors. *I Studied Inscriptions from before the Flood: Ancient Near Eastern, Literary, and Linguistic Approaches to Genesis 1–11.* Sources for Biblical and Theological Study 4. Winona Lake, IN: Eisenbrauns, 1994.

Huffmon, Herbert B. "Delitzsch, Friedrich." In *Dictionary of Biblical Interpretation*, edited by John H. Hayes, 1:267. Nashville: Abingdon, 1999.

Keil, C. F., and Franz Delitzsch. *Biblical Commentary on the Old Testament.* 25 vols. Translated by James Martin. Grand Rapids: Eerdmans, 1949.

Lewis, Theodore J. "Dead, Abode of the." In *ABD* 2:101–5.

Maiberger, Paul, and Christoph Dohmen. "סיני *sinay*." In *TDOT* 10 (1999) 216–35.

Martin, Harriet P. *Fara: A Reconstruction of the Ancient Mesopotamian City of Shuruppak.* Birmingham, UK: Chris Martin, 1988.

Martin, Luther, and Anita Maria Leopold. "New Approaches to the Study of Syncretism." In *New Approaches to the Study of Religion, Volume 2: Textual, Comparative, Sociological, and Cognitive Approaches*, edited by Peter Antes et al., 93–108. Berlin: de Gruyter, 2004.

Meek, Th. J. "The Code of Hammurabi." In *ANET*, 169–80.

Meier, Samuel A. "Angel I." In *DDD*, 45–50.

————. "Hammurapi." In *ABD*, 3:39–42.

Mettinger, T. N. D. "Cherubim." In *DDD*, 189–92.

————. "Seraphim." In *DDD*, 742–44.

Metzger, Bruce M. *A Textual Commentary on the Greek New Testament.* 2nd ed. London: United Bible Societies, 1994.

Millard, A. R. "Nabû." In *DDD*, 607–10.

Miller, Patrick D. "Aspects of Religion at Ugarit." In *AIR*, 53–66.

————. *The Religion of Ancient Israel*. Library of Ancient Israel. Louisville: Westminster John Knox, 2000.

————, Paul D. Hanson, and S. Dean McBride, editors. *Ancient Israelite Religion: Essays in Honor of Frank Moore Cross*. Philadelphia: Fortress, 1987.

Moran, William L., editor and translator. *The Amarna Letters*. Baltimore: John Hopkins University Press, 1992.

Nickelsburg, George W. E. "Son of Man." In *DDD*, 800–804.

Oden, Robert A. *The Bible without Theology: The Theological Tradition and Alternatives to It*. 1987. Reprinted, Urbana: University of Illinois Press, 2000.

Paden, William E. "Comparison in the Study of Religion." In *New Approaches to the Study of Religion, Volume 2: Textual, Comparative, Sociological, and Cognitive Approaches*, edited by Peter Antes et al., 77–92. Berlin: de Gruyter, 2004.

Peckham, Brian. "Phoenicia and the Religion of Israel." In *AIR*, 79–99.

Perlitt, Lothar. "Sinai und Horeb." In *Beiträge zur alttestamentlichen Theologie: Festschrift für Walther Zimmerli zum 70. Geburtstag*, edited by Herbert Donner et al., 302–22. Göttingen: Vandenhoeck & Ruprecht, 1977.

Pope, Marvin H. *El in the Ugaritic Texts*. Vetus Testamentum Supplements 2. Leiden: Brill, 1955.

Pritchard, James B., editor. *Ancient Near Eastern Texts Relating to the Old Testament*. 3rd ed. Princeton: Princeton University Press, 1969.

Richardson, M. E. J. *Hammurabi's Laws: Text, Translation and Glossary*. Biblical Seminar 73. Sheffield: Sheffield Academic, 2000.

Roth, Martha. "The Laws of Hammurabi." In *COS*, 2:335–53.

Rummel, Stan, editor. *Ras Shamra Parallels: The Texts from Ugarit and the Hebrew Bible*. Vol. 3. AnOr 51. Rome: Pontifical Biblical Institute Press, 1982.

Shavit, Yaacov, and Mordechai Eran. *The Hebrew Bible Reborn: A History of Biblical Culture and the Battles over the Bible in Modern Judaism*. Translated by Chaya Naor. Studia Judaica 38. Berlin: de Gruyter, 2007.

Smith, Mark S. *The Origins of Monotheism: Israel's Polytheistic Background and the Ugaritic Texts*. Oxford: Oxford University Press, 2002.

Speiser, E. A. "The Creation Epic." In *ANET*, 60–72, 501–3.

————. "The Gilgamesh Epic." In *ANET*, 72–99.

Tigay, Jeffrey H. *The Evolution of the Gilgamesh Epic*. 1982. Reprinted, Wauconda, IL: Bolchazzy-Carducci, 2002.

Toorn, Karel van der et al., editors. *Dictionary of Deities and Demons in the Bible*. 2nd ed. Leiden: Brill, 1999.

————. "Yahweh." In *DDD*, 910–19.

Walton, John H. *Ancient Israelite Literature in Its Cultural Context.* 2nd corrected ed. Grand Rapids: Zondervan, 1990.

———. *The Ancient Near East and the Old Testament: Introducing the Conceptual World of the Hebrew Bible.* Grand Rapids: Baker Academic, 2006.

Younger, K. Lawson et al., editors. *The Biblical Canon in Comparative Perspective.* Scripture in Context 4. Ancient Near Eastern Texts and Studies 11. Lewiston, NY: Mellen, 1991.

Additional Materials on the Babel–Bible Conflict

Barth, Jakob. *Babel und israelitisches Religionswesen: Vortrag.* Berlin: Mayer & Müller, 1902.

Baumgartner, Walther. "Babylonien: III. Babel und Bibel." In *Die Religion in Geschichte und Gegenwart,* edited by Hermann Gunkel and Leopold Zscharnack, 1:714–18. 2nd ed. Tübingen: Mohr/Siebeck, 1927.

Chavalas, Mark W. "Assyriology and Biblical Studies: A Century and a Half of Tension." In *Mesopotamia and the Bible: Comparative Explorations,* edited by Mark W. Chavalas and K. Lawson Younger Jr., 21–67. New York: T. & T. Clark, 2003.

Döller, Johannes. *Bibel und Babel oder Babel und Bibel? Eine Entgegnung aug Friedrich Delitzsch' "Babel und Bibel."* Paderborn: Schöningh, 1903.

Ebach, J. "Babel und Bibel oder: Das 'Heidnische' im Alten Testament." In *Restauration der Götter: Antike Religion und Neo-Paganismus,* edited by Richard Faber and Renate Schlesier, 26–44. Würzburg: Königshausen & Neumann, 1986.

Finkelstein, Jacob L. "Bible and Babel: A Comparative Study of the Hebrew and Babylonian Religious Spirit." *Commentary* 26 (1958) 431–44.

Gasser, J. C. *Babel und Bibel.* Schaffhausen: Kühn, 1903.

Giesebrecht, Friedrich. *Friede für Babel und Bibel.* Königsberg: Thomas & Opermann, 1903.

Goldschmied, Leopold. *Der Kampf um Babel-Bibel im Lichte des Judentums.* Frankfurt: Kauffman, 1903.

Harnack, Adolf. *Letter to the "Preussische Jahrbücher" on the German Emperor's Criticism of Prof. Delitzsch's Lectures on "Babel and Bible."* Translated by Thomas Bailey Saunders. London: Williams & Norgate, 1903.

Hommel, Fritz. *Die altorientalischen Denkmäler und das Alter Testament: Eine Erwiderung auf Prof. Fr. Delitzsch's "Babel und Bibel."* 2nd ed. Berlin: Deutsche Orient Mission, 1903.

Horovitz, Jacob. *Babel und Bibel: Randglossen zu den beiden Vorträgen Friedrich Delitzschs.* Frankfurt: Kauffmann, 1904.

Huffmon, Herbert B. "Babel und Bibel: The Encounter between Babylon and the Bible." *Michigan Quarterly Review* 22 (1983) 309–20. Reprinted in *Backgrounds for the Bible,* edited by Michael Patrick O'Connor and David Noel Freedman. Winona Lake, IN: Eisenbrauns, 1987.

———. "Babel und Bibel." In *Dictionary of Biblical Interpretation,* edited by John H. Hayes, 1:92. Nashville: Abingdon, 1999.

Jeremias, Alfred. *Im Kampfe um Babel und Bibel: Ein Wort zur Verständigung und Abwehr.* 4th ed. Leipzig: Hinrichs, 1903.

Johanning, Klaus. *Der Bibel-Babel-Streit: Eine forschungsgeschichtliche Studie.* Europäische Hochschulschriften 343. Frankfurt: Lang, 1988.

Kittel, Rudolf. *Die babylonischen Ausgrabungen und die biblische Urgeschichte.* 4th ed. Leipzig: Deichert, 1903.

Klausner, M. A. *Hie Babel, Hie Bibel! Anmerkungen zu des Professors Delitzsch zweitem Vortrag über Babel und Bibel.* 3rd ed. Berlin: Calvary, 1903.

———. *Professor Delitzsch: Eine Erwiderung.* Berlin: Verlag der "Israelitschen Wochenschrift," 1904.

Knieschke, W. *Bibel und Babel El und Bel: Eine Replik auf Friedrich Delitzschs Babel und Bibel.* Berlin: Faber, 1902.

Köberle, Justus. *Babylonische Kultur und biblische Religion: Ein erweiterter Vortrag.* Munich: Beck, 1903.

König, Eduard. *The Bible and Babylon: Their Relationship in the History of Culture.* Translated by William Turnbull Pilter. London: Religious Tract Society, 1905.

Larsen, Mogens Trolle. "The 'Babel/Bible' Controversy and Its Aftermath." In *Civilizations of the Ancient Near East,* edited by Jack M. Sasson, 1:95–106. New York: Scribners, 1995.

Lehmann, Reinhard G. *Friedrich Delitzsch und der Babel–Bibel Streit.* Orbis biblicus et orientalis 133. Göttingen: Vandenhoeck & Ruprecht, 1994.

Liwak, Rüdiger. "Bibel und Babel: Wider die theologische und religionsgeschichtliche Naivität." *Berliner Theologische Zeitung* 15 (1998) 206–30.

Meyer, S. A. *Contra Delitzsch! Die Babel-Hypothesen widerlegt.* Frankfurt: Kauffmann, 1903.

Münz, Wilhelm. *"Es werde Lichte!" Eine Aufklärung über Bibel und Babel.* Breslau: Koebner, 1903.

Oettli, Samuel. *Der Kampf um Bibel und Babel.* Leipzig: Deichert, 1903.

Porges, Nathan. *Bibelkunde und Babelfunde: Eine Kritische Besprechung von Friedrich Delitzsch's Babel und Bibel*. Leipzig: Liebes & Teichtner, 1903.

Rosenthal, Ludwig A. *Babel und Bibel oder Babel gegen Bibel? Ein Wort zur Klärung*. 2nd ed. Berlin: Boppelauer, 1903.

Schmidt, G. *Babel und Bibel: Apologetilcher Vortrag*. Königsberg: Gräfe & Unzer, 1903.

Schreiber, Emilio. *Bibbia e Babele: Appunti alle Conferenze del Prof. Gustavo Sacerdoti*. Trieste: Morterra, 1904.

Söderblom, Nathan. *Uppenbarelsereligion: Några Synpunkter I anledning af Babel-Bibeldiskussion*. Uppsala: Schultz, 1903.

Sommer, Bruno. *Biblische Geschichtslügen: Ein Beitrag zur Babel-Bibel-Frage und eine volksverständliche Anleitung zur Bibel-Beurteilung*. Bamberg: Handel, 1903.

Toy, Crawford. "Panbabylonianism." *Harvard Theological Review* 3 (1910) 47–84.

Volck, Wilhelm. *Zum Kampf um Bibel und Babel: Noch ein Wort zur Verständigung und Abwehr*. Rostock: Stiller, 1903.

Vries, Jan de. "Panbabylonianism." In *The Study of Religion: A Historical Approach*, 95–98. Translated with an introduction by Kees W. Bolle. New York: Harcourt Brace & World, 1967.

Index of Ancient Documents

∾

Index of Ancient Personal Names, Divine Names, and Place Names

Index of Authors

www.ingramcontent.com/pod-product-compliance
Lightning Source LLC
Chambersburg PA
CBHW030851090426
42737CB00009B/1185